THE FIRST CHURCH OF CHRIST IN LANCASTER,
MASSACHUSETTS, ORGANIZED 1653

Interior of the Fifth Meetinghouse of the First Church, 1816

The
Colonial Clergy of Maryland, Delaware and Georgia

By

FREDERICK LEWIS WEIS, TH.D.

*Minister of the First Church
of Christ in Lancaster*

Southern Historical Press, Inc.
Greenville, South Carolina

This volume was reproduced from
A personal copy located in the
Publisher's private library

All rights reserved. No part of this publication may be reproduced,
stored in a retrieval system, transmitted in any form, posted
on to the web in any form or by any means without
the prior written permission of the publisher.

Please direct all correspondence and orders to:

www.southernhistoricalpress.com
or
**SOUTHERN HISTORICAL PRESS, Inc.
PO BOX 1267
Greenville, SC   29601
southernhistoricalpress@gmail.com**

Originally published: Lancaster, MA.   1950
Copyright 1950 by: Frederick L. Weis
ISBN #978-1-63914-025-1
All rights Reserved.
Printed in the United States of America

CONTENTS

Interior of the First Church in Lancaster . . . . . *Frontispiece*
Publications of the Society 4
List of Annual Addresses, 1934-1950 7
The Colonial Clergy of America 9
Officers of the Society, 1933-1950 11
Members of the Council, 1933-1950 12
Membership, 1933-1950 14
The Colonial Clergy of Maryland, 1629-1776 31
The Colonial Clergy of Delaware, 1638-1776 71
The Colonial Clergy of Georgia, 1733-1776 89
The Colonial Churches of Maryland, 1629-1776 94
Friends Meetings in Maryland, 1656-1776 99
The Colonial Churches of Delaware, 1638-1776 101
The Colonial Churches of Georgia, 1733-1776 103
Summary of the Colonial Clergy and the Colonial Churches of
   Maryland, Delaware and Georgia 104

LIST OF ANNUAL ADDRESSES DELIVERED BEFORE THE SOCIETY OF THE DESCENDANTS OF THE COLONIAL CLERGY
1934-1950

1934 "The Reverend Samuel Skelton, A.M., 1593-1634." By The Honorable Herbert Parker, LL.D.

1935 "The Beginnings of the Great Awakening, 1735." By The Reverend Charles Edwards Park, D.D.

1936 "The Mayhew Oligarchy." By The Reverend Abbot Peterson, D.D.

1937 "The New England Clergy in the Glacial Age." By Clifford Kenyon Shipton, Ph.D.

1938 "The Reverend George Phillips, A.M., First Minister at Watertown, 1630-1644." By The Reverend Henry Wilder Foote, D.D.

1939 "Tohatawan, Chief of the Nashoba Praying Indians." By The Reverend John Henry Wilson.

1940 "The Reverend Walter Powers, Separatist." By Mr. Arthur Clark Harrington.

1941 "The Reverend John Eliot, Apostle to the Indians." By The Reverend Louis Craig Cornish, D.D.

1942 "The Reverend John Miller, A.B., 1604-1663, First Minister at Groton."
"The Reverend William Tompson, A.B., 1598-1666, First Minister at Quincy."
"The Reverend Ralph Wheelock, A.M., 1600-1684, of Dedham and Medfield."

1944 "Isaac Backus, Pioneer for Religious Liberty." By the Reverend Richard Donald Pierce, Ph.D.

1945 "The Reverend Thomas Hooker, First Minister at Cambridge, Massachusetts and Hartford, Connecticut." By Mrs. Marion Fuller Safford.

1946 "The Church in Cambridge and Its First Two Ministers." By The Reverend Samuel Atkins Eliot, D.D., LL.D.

1947 "The Significance of Puritanism in Modern Democracy." By Clifford Kenyon Shipton, Ph.D.

ANNUAL ADDRESSES

1948 "The Reverend William Tompson, A.B., the First Minister of the First Church in Braintree (now Quincy), 1639-1666." By Mr. Ralph Newell Thompson.

1949 "The New England Company of 1649 and its Missionary Work among the Indians." By The Reverend Frederick Lewis Weis, Th.D.

1950 "The First Church of Westford, Massachusetts, 1727-1950." By The Reverend John Boynton Wilson Day.

THE COLONIAL CLERGY OF AMERICA

THE history of the towns of the British Colonies in North America during the colonial period was in large measure that of their churches, and the history of these churches was largely that of their clergy. The ministers of that period were the leaders in theology, law, medicine, education, and to a considerable degree, in politics and Indian warfare. Often they were the only educated persons in a community.

Harvard College was founded in 1636 to provide a literate ministry for the churches of New England, and it is to be noted that of the thousand colonial ministers in Massachusetts nine-tenths of them were college graduates and many others were privately tutored by college-trained clergymen.

The Society of the Descendants of the Colonial Clergy was incorporated by the Commonwealth of Massachusetts, on February 9, 1933. Its major purposes are "to cherish and maintain the memory of the lives and works of the colonial clergy of America; to perpetuate their spirit and the religious freedom which they sought in the New World; to keep in remembrance the churches which they served; to promote the fitting celebration of anniversaries both of colonial ecclesiastical bodies and churches and of events in the lives of their clergy; to collect and preserve documents, histories, biographical sketches and memorials pertaining to the colonial clergy of America and the parishes which they served; and to promote social intercourse and friendship among the descendants of the colonial clergy now and hereafter."

The first endeavor of the founders of these colonies, which later formed the United States of America, was the continuance of the Christian institutions under which they had been born. As Francis Baylies said: "The clergy were the principal instruments in keeping alive the spirit and enterprise of the English race in the wilds of America. Nor did they confine themselves to ecclesiastical functions. Their influence was felt in the civil affairs of Government, and even in the transactions of ordinary life."

There were nearly five thousand settled ministers in colonial America, each of whom, according to his ability, education and station, was an unquestioned leader in his time and place. With the passage of many decades some of the ancient parishes which they served have ceased to exist; many are still strong and flourishing. It is to ensure the perpetuation of the memory of these leaders of colonial times, the founders and shapers of our national character and institutions, that this Society of the Descendants of the Colonial Clergy was formed.

Eligibility

"Any person shall be eligible for membership who is at least twenty-one years of age, and a lineal descendant of an ancestor who was a clergyman regularly ordained, installed or settled over any Christian church within the limits of the thirteen colonies prior to July 4, 1776."—*From the By-laws.*

The Society includes the descendants of Colonial Clergymen of all denominations.

OFFICERS OF THE SOCIETY
1933-1950

Governors General
1933 THE REVEREND HENRY WILDER FOOTE, D.D. 1947
1948 MAJOR DUNCAN FORBES THAYER 1949
FRANKLIN HASKINS PERKINS, M.D.

Deputy-Governors General
1933 COLONEL JOHN ELIOT THAYER 1933
1933 WILLIAM CROWNINSHIELD ENDICOTT 1936
1936 THE REVEREND ENDICOTT PEABODY, D.D. 1944
1945 THE HONORABLE LEVERETT SALTONSTALL, LL.D. 1950
GEORGE WILLIAM WHEELWRIGHT III

Secretary General
DUDLEY HUNTINGTON DORR, ESQUIRE

Historian General
THE REVEREND FREDERICK LEWIS WEIS, Th.D.

Treasurers General
1933 WILLIAM DEXTER, ESQUIRE 1940
1940 FRANKLIN HASKINS PERKINS, M.D. 1949
FRANCIS WILSON FLEISCHNER

Chaplains General
1933 THE REVEREND LOUIS CRAIG CORNISH, D.D. 1950
THE REVEREND JOHN HENRY WILSON

Chancellors General
1933 THE HONORABLE HERBERT PARKER, LL.D. 1939
1939 THE HONORABLE ALEXANDER RADCLIFFE MACDONELL 1950
MAJOR HAVEN PARKER

Marshal General
COLONEL GEORGE ALANSON PARKER

OFFICERS OF THE SOCIETY

Surgeon General
FRANKLIN GREENE BALCH, M.D.

Signets General
1933 THE REVEREND RICHARD ALLEN DAY 1942
LIEUTENANT RICHARD GIBSON DORR

Members of the Council

1948-1951	PROFESSOR ARTHUR ADAMS, Ph.D., D.D.
1935-1938	THE HONORABLE CHARLES FRANCIS ADAMS, LL.D.
1936-1939	THE REV. ALFRED WILLIAMS ANTHONY, D.D., LL.D.†
1949-1950	THE REVEREND EVERETT MOORE BAKER, D.D.†
1936-1939	JOHN WASHBURN BARTOL, M.D.†
1933-1939	HENRY FORBES BIGELOW
1941-1944	JOHN CHANDLER
1945-1948	CHARLES BENSON CHICKERING
1950-1952	THE REVEREND FRANK BYRON CRANDALL
1934-1937	THE REVEREND CHRISTOPHER RHODES ELIOT, LL.D.†
1937-1940	THE REVEREND SAMUEL ATKINS ELIOT, D.D., LL.D.†
1946-1949	THE REVEREND DAN HUNTINGTON FENN
1933-1936	FRANCIS ABBOT GOODHUE, ESQUIRE
1942-1945	GEORGE CHEEVER GUILD
1941-1944	JOSEPH ALFRED HARWOOD†
1942-1945	GEORGE ELI HOWE, ESQUIRE†
1946-1949	THE REVEREND WILLIAM SAFFORD JONES, D.D.
1940-1941	THE REVEREND AUGUSTUS MENDON LORD, D.D.†
1950-1953	EDWARD CRARY LORD
1944-1950	RALPH LOWELL, ESQUIRE
1944-1946	MRS. GEORGE HENRY MAY
1938-1941	GEORGE PARSONS MILMINE
1947-1950	THE RIGHT REVEREND NORMAN BURDETT NASH, D.D.
1937-1940	THE REVEREND MORGAN PHELPS NOYES, D.D.
1933-1936	THE REVEREND CHARLES EDWARDS PARK, D.D.
1939-1940	FRANKLIN HASKINS PERKINS, M.D.
1941-1943	THE VERY REVEREND HOWARD DELVON PERKINS
1944-1947	THE REVEREND RICHARD DONALD PIERCE, Ph.D.
1945-1948	MRS. MURRAY ANTHONY POTTER
1935-1938	THE VERY REVEREND HOWARD CHANDLER ROBBINS, D.D.
1940-1946	ARTHUR DEBERDT ROBINS
1938-1941	THE REVEREND SYDNEY BRUCE SNOW, D.D., Ph.D.†
1940-1942	THE RT. REV. W. BERTRAND STEVENS, D.D., LL.D.†

OFFICERS OF THE SOCIETY

1939-1942   GENERAL CHARLES PELOT SUMMERALL, LL.D., D.Mil.Sc.
1950-1953   ALDRICH TAYLOR
1934-1937   MRS. BAYARD THAYER†
1933-1934   MAJOR DUNCAN FORBES THAYER
1949-1952   THE HONORABLE JOHN ELIOT THAYER, JR.
1934-1934   MRS. NATHANIEL THAYER†
1933-1934   GEORGE WILLIAM WHEELWRIGHT, III
1933-1935   THE REVEREND JOHN HENRY WILSON
1948-1951   COMMANDER WALTER MUIR WHITEHILL, Ph.D.

Honorary Members

JAMES ROWLAND ANGELL, Litt.D., LL.D.†
THE REVEREND GEORGE MACLAREN BRYDEN, D.D.
JAMES BRYANT CONANT, Ph.D., LL.D.
THE REVEREND SAMUEL ATKINS ELIOT, D.D., LL.D.†
ABBOTT LAWRENCE LOWELL, LL.D., Ph.D., Litt.D.†
THE HONORABLE LEVERETT SALTONSTALL, LL.D.
CHARLES SEYMOUR, Ph.D., Litt.D., LL.D.

MEMBERSHIP

(Note: One ancestor for each member is listed here.)

305* ABBOTT, MRS. GEORGE ANDREWS, Oak Park, Ill.
8th from Rev. Laurentius Van Gaasbeck of Kingston, N. Y.

299* ADAMS, PROF. ARTHUR, Ph.D., D.D., Hartford, Conn.
4th from (Rev.) Mary Garwood of Egg Harbor, N. J.

121* ADAMS, HON. CHARLES FRANCIS, LL.D., Boston.
9th from Rev. John Cotton of Boston.

90* ALLEN, MRS. WILLIAM PORTER, Irvington, N. J.
9th from Rev. Johann Theodorus Polhemius of New York.

200† ANGELL, JAMES ROWLAND, Litt.D., LL.D., New Haven, Conn. (Died March 4, 1949.)
8th from Rev. Chad Brown of Providence, R. I.

50† ANTHONY, REV. ALFRED WILLIAMS, D.D., LL.D., Lewiston, Me. (Died January 18, 1939.)
8th from Rev. Chad Brown of Providence, R. I.

280 AULD, MISS LULU GRAY, Danville, Va.
6th from Rev. Peter Fontaine of King William Parish, Va.

51† AUSTIN, MRS. EDWARD, Milwaukee, Wis. (Died March 3, 1950.)
10th from Rev. John Lothrop of Scituate.

159† BAKER, REV. EVERETT MOORE, D.D., Wellesley Hills. (Died August 31, 1950.)
6th from Rev. Robert Jordon of Middletown, Va.

70* BAKER, MISS LUCY MYRTLE, Templeton.
8th from Rev. Ralph Wheelock of Medfield.

71* BAKER, MISS MARY LEONA, Templeton.
8th from Rev. Ralph Wheelock of Medfield.

76* BALCH, FRANKLIN GREENE, M.D., Jamaica Plain.
8th from Rev. Samuel Gorton of Warwick, R. I.

256* BARRINGTON, MRS. LAURENCE WALKER LIVINGSTON, Worcester.
8th from Rev. John Eliot of Roxbury.

236 BARTER, MRS. ARTHUR EVERETT, Roslindale.
8th from Rev. Nathaniel Rogers of Ipswich.

57† BARTOL, JOHN WASHBURN, M.D., Milton. (Died November 14, 1950.)
7th from Rev. John Wheelwright of Salisbury.

157 BATCHELDER, MISS ANN, Larchmont, N. Y.
9th from Rev. George Phillips of Watertown.

295* BATH, MRS. JOHN CHESTER, Worcester.
9th from Rev. William Walton of Marblehead.

MEMBERSHIP

86*   BATTLE, MRS. SAMUEL WESTRAY, Asheville, N. C.
         10th from Rev. Joseph Hull of Weymouth.

326*   BENNETT, MRS. JOHN HARRINGTON, Worcester.
         9th from Rev. Thomas Carter of Woburn.

27*   BIGELOW, HENRY FORBES, Bolton.
         10th from Rev. John Miller of Yarmouth.

237   BISELL, MRS. WILLIAM CORYELL, Circleville, Ohio.
         5th from Rev. Tobias Wagner of Reading, Pa.

186†   BLACK, MRS. WILMER, Towson, Md. (Died March 5, 1945.)
         9th from Rev. Everardus Bogardus of New York.

258   BODEN, HARRY CLARK, IV, Newark, Del.
         9th from Rev. Peter Prudden of Milford, Conn.

262*   BODEN, MRS. HARRY CLARK, Newark, Del.
         9th from Rev. John Woodbridge of Andover.

325   BOGARDUS, MISS CAROLA WINIFRED CORSON, Hillside, N. J.
         8th from Rev. Everardus Bogardus of New York.

126*   BOOTH, FRANCIS MILLET, Urbanna, Va.
         11th from Rev. John Eliot of Roxbury.

79*   BOOTH, MRS. WILLIAM HARRIS, Urbanna, Va.
         10th from Rev. John Eliot of Roxbury.

100*   BOURNE, MRS. STANDISH TABER, JR., Scotia, N. Y.
         12th from Elder William Brewster of Plymouth.

267   BOYLE, MRS. PAUL EDMUND, Weston.
         7th from Rev. Joseph Coit of Plainfield, Conn.

68†   BRACKETT, JEFFREY RICHARDSON, Ph.D., Peterborough, N. H. (Died December 4, 1949.)
         9th from Rev. William Tompson of Braintree.

117*   BRADFORD, MISS MARJORIE CROSS, Putnam, Conn.
         8th from Rev. Nehemiah Smith of New London, Conn.

250   BRANDON, MISS LOUISE MILLIKEN, Portland, Me.
         9th from Rev. John Wheelwright of Exeter, N. H.

209   BROWN, MRS. HARRY ALVIN, Needham.
         10th from Rev. Samuel Whiting of Lynn.

306   BRUINGTON, JAMES CLARKE, Pensacola, Fla.
         6th from Rev. William Murphy of Staunton, Va.

324*   BRYDON, REV. GEORGE MACLAREN, D.D., Richmond, Va.
         8th from Rev. Charles Grymes of York Parish, Va.

119*   BURLEY, MRS. BENJAMIN THOMAS, Worcester.
         12th from Rev. Stephen Bachiller of Lynn.

65*   CALDER, PHILIP RAYMOND, Boston.
         10th from Rev. William Worcester of Salisbury.

80*   CAREY, MRS. ARTHUR GRAHAM, Cambridge.
         10th from Rev. John Eliot of Roxbury.

128*   CAREY, CHRISTOPHER MILLET, Cambridge.
         11th from Rev. John Eliot of Roxbury.

129*   CAREY, MISS HILDA, Cambridge.
         11th from Rev. John Eliot of Roxbury.

290   CARLOCK, MRS. LYMAN JUDY, Oak Park, Ill.
         5th from Rev. Robert Elkin of Va. and Ky.

272*	CARLSON, MRS. JOHN LUND, White Sulphur Springs, Mont. 4th from Rev. Nathan Howard of Waterford, Conn.
319	CARMAN, MISS BESSIE CLIFTON, Chicago, Ill. 6th from Rev. Joshua Herring of Bear Creek, N. C.
73*	CARPENTER, MRS. CLOVIS LEON, Worcester. 11th from Rev. Robert Peck of Hingham.
265	CARR, MRS. RAYMOND STUART, La Grange, Ill. 8th from Rev. Hugh Mosher of Tiverton, R. I.
67†	CARTER, MRS. MILES LEACH, Attleborough. (Died September 9, 1946.) 6th from Rev. Ebenezer Jenckes of Providence, R. I.
146*	CHANDLER, JOHN, Sterling. 9th from Rev. Thomas Carter of Woburn.
131*	CHERRY, MRS. LEWIS WILLIAMSON, Little Rock, Ark. 7th from Rev. James Noyes of Newbury.
167	CHICKERING, CHARLES BENSON, Lancaster. 7th from Rev. Francis Dane of Andover.
160	CLAPP, RICHARD FLETCHER, Gill. 10th from Rev. Stephen Bachiller of Lynn.
270	CLARK, MISS CLARIBEL MAE COLEMAN, Flint, Mich. 10th from Rev. Jonathan Burr of Dorchester.
314	CLIFTON, MRS. LUCIUS ALLEN, Fulton, Ky. 7th from Rev. James Boisseau of King and Queen Parish, Va.
269	COLEMAN, MISS ELIZABETH MAE, Flint, Mich. 9th from Rev. Adam Blakeman of Stratford, Conn.
137R	COLLIN, MRS. CHARLES RUSSELL, Mt. Pleasant, Mich. 10th from Rev. John Mayo of Boston.
201*	CONANT, PRESIDENT JAMES BRYANT, Ph.D., LL.D., Cambridge. 8th from Rev. William Walton of Marblehead.
247	COOK, ROSS KEELYE, East Orange, N. J. 8th from Rev. Lawrence Karlsson Lock of Wilmington, Del.
116*	COOLIDGE, MISS H. ELIZABETH, Framingham. 6th from Rev. John Prentice of Lancaster.
140	COOPER, EUGENE SMITH, Dayton, Ohio. 10th from Rev. Joseph Hull of Weymouth.
5†	CORNISH, REV. LOUIS CRAIG, D.D., D.Pol.Sc., Harvard. (Died January 7, 1950.) 9th from Elder William Brewster of Plymouth.
220	CRAFT, MRS. AUGUSTUS, New Orleans, La. 6th from Rev. Robert Jordon of Middletown, Va.
339	CRANDALL, REV. FRANK BYRON, Salem. 7th from Rev. Joseph Crandall of Westerly, R. I.
196†	CRANDALL, MISS IRENE JEAN, Chicago, Ill. (Died May 28, 1940.) 9th from Rev. Nicholas Street of Taunton.
192	CRAWFORD, MRS. SETH TURNER, Boston. 10th from Rev. Stephen Bachiller of Lynn.

MEMBERSHIP

83† CRUFT, MISS FRANCES CORDIS, Boston. (Died August 22, 1941.)
    10th from Rev. Nathaniel Ward of Ipswich.

313 CRUTCHER, MISS EMMA KEATS, Louisville, Ky.
    7th from Rev. James Boisseau of King and Queen Parish, Va.

312 CRUTCHER, MRS. PHILIP SPEED, Louisville, Ky.
    6th from Rev. James Boisseau of King and Queen Parish, Va.

106† CULVER, MRS. FRED WILLIAM, Saginaw, Mich. (Died February 8, 1937.)
    9th from Rev. John Cotton of Boston.

145R CUMMINS, MRS. ALEXANDER GRISWOLD, Poughkeepsie, N. Y.
    9th from Rev. John Lothrop of Scituate.

127* CUNNINGHAM, MRS. MICHAEL M., Cambridge.
    11th from Rev. John Eliot of Roxbury.

193R DANSEY, MRS. JAMES WILLIAM, Chicago, Ill.
    6th from Rev. William Murphy of Staunton, Va.

266 DAVIS, EDMUND EUGENE, Wilmington, Del.
    9th from Rev. Thomas Hanford of Norwalk, Conn.

4* DAY, REV. RICHARD ALLEN, Peterborough, N. H.
    11th from Elder William Brewster of Plymouth.

13* DAY, MRS. RICHARD ALLEN, Peterborough, N. H.
    10th from Rev. Stephen Bachiller of Lynn.

197* DEAN, MISS ELLA ROSE, Bridgeport, Ill.
    7th from Rev. Michael Wigglesworth of Malden.

234* DEEBLE, MISS ELIZABETH, Washington, D. C.
    10th from Rev. John Lothrop of Barnstable.

240* DEGROOT, MISS ADELAIDE MILTON, New York, N. Y.
    8th from Rev. Francis Higginson of Salem.

141† DEWSON, EDWARD HENRY, Boothbay Harbor, Me. (Died February 9, 1939.)
    9th from Rev. William Tompson of Braintree.

153R DEWSON, MISS MARY WILLIAMS, Castine, Me.
    9th from Rev. William Tompson of Braintree.

17† DEXTER, WILLIAM, Lancaster. (Died February 8, 1943.)
    10th from Rev. Peter Bulkeley of Concord.

18* DEXTER, MRS. WILLIAM, Lancaster.
    9th from Rev. Nathaniel Ward of Ipswich.

94* DEXTER, MISS MARY ANN, Lancaster.
    11th from Rev. Peter Bulkeley of Concord.

92* DEXTER, NATHANIEL THAYER, Lancaster.
    11th from Rev. Peter Bulkeley of Concord.

93* DEXTER, PHILIP, 2ND., Lancaster.
    11th from Rev. Peter Bulkeley of Concord.

52 DEXTER, ROBERT CLOUTMAN, Ph.D., Belmont.
    10th from Rev. Peter Hobart of Hingham.

53 DEXTER, MRS. ROBERT CLOUTMAN, Ph.D., Belmont.
    10th from Rev. Roger Williams of Providence, R. I.

MEMBERSHIP

99*   DIK, MRS. WILLARD B., Wayland.
       7th from Rev. John Prentice of Lancaster.

96†   DORMAN, MRS. H. LOUIS, Akron, Ohio. (Died January 31, 1937.)
       11th from Rev. Ralph Partridge of Duxbury.

3*   DORR, DUDLEY HUNTINGTON, Lancaster.
       9th from Rev. Robert Gutch of Pemequid, Me.

101*   DORR, DUDLEY HUNTINGTON, JR., Lancaster.
       8th from Rev. Thomas Buckingham of Saybrook, Conn.

243*   DORR, MRS. DUDLEY HUNTINGTON, JR., Lancaster.
       10th from Elder William Brewster of Plymouth.

227*   DORR, LIEUTENANT RICHARD GIBSON, Boston.
       10th from Rev. Robert Gutch of Pemequid, Me.

195R   DRAKE, EDWIN HOWARD, Lincoln, Neb.
       8th from Rev. James Keith of Bridgewater.

213   DUDLEY, ROLAND OSCAR, Huntington Park, Calif.
       9th from Rev. Samuel Dudley of Exeter, N. H.

253   DUPONT, MRS. EUGENE, Greenville, Del.
       5th from Rev. John William Kurtz of Tulpehocken, Pa.

315   EATON, CLARENCE ELERY, Portland, Me.
       9th from Rev. Thomas Mayhew of Edgartown.

244   EDDY, MISS HARRIETTE WELLINGTON, Worcester.
       7th from Rev. George Phillips of Watertown.

44†   ELIOT, REV. CHRISTOPHER RHODES, LL.D., Cambridge. (Died June, 1945.)
       8th from Rev. Thomas Shephard of Cambridge.

47†   ELIOT, REV. SAMUEL ATKINS, D.D., LL.D., Cambridge. (Died October 15, 1950.)
       6th from Rev. Nathaniel Gookin of Cambridge.

331   ELLIOTT, MRS. HARRY, Sausalito, Calif.
       9th from Rev. John Warham of Dorchester.

105†   EMERY, MISS AMY ETHEL, Brookline. (Died June 26, 1949.)
       11th from Rev. Stephen Bachiller of Lynn.

84†   ENDICOTT, WILLIAM CROWNINSHIELD, Danvers. (Died November 28, 1936.)
       9th from Rev. Samuel Skelton of Salem.

214†   ERIKSSON, MRS. AUGUST, Los Angeles, Calif. (Died July 27, 1941.)
       11th from Elder William Brewster of Plymouth.

55†   FELTON, EDGAR CONWAY, Haverford, Pa. (Died September 18, 1937.)
       9th from Rev. William Walton of Marblehead.

21   FENN, REV. DAN HUNTINGTON, Cambridge.
       8th from Rev. John Whiting of Hartford, Conn.

284*   FLEISCHNER, FRANCIS WILSON, Lancaster.
       9th from Rev. Peter Bulkeley of Concord.

219   FLETCHER, HENRY, Greenwich, Conn.
       8th from Rev. Samuel Dudley of Exeter, N. H.

150   FLETCHER, ROLAND WILLARD, Winchester.
       8th from Rev. Samuel Stow of Middletown, Conn.

109*	FOLGER, WALTER WESTON, Chattanooga, Tenn.	

- 109* FOLGER, WALTER WESTON, Chattanooga, Tenn.
  11th from Rev. Stephen Bachiller of Lynn.
- 9* FOOTE, REV. HENRY WILDER, D.D., S.T.D., Cambridge.
  8th from Rev. George Phillips of Watertown.
- 191R FORNOF, MRS. JOHN RENCHIN, Streator, Ill.
  10th from Rev. Joseph Hull of Weymouth.
- 333 FOSTER, SYDNEY HILL, Oakland, Calif.
  9th from Rev. Henry Flynt of Braintree.
- 61* FRISSELL, MRS. GLENVILLE COLLINS, Miami, Fla.
  9th from Rev. Samuel Newman of Rehoboth, Mass.
- 42† FUESS, MRS. CLAUDE MOORE, Andover. (Died July 26, 1943.)
  11th from Rev. Stephen Bachiller of Lynn.
- 233 GAIR, COLIN MUNRO, Los Angeles, Calif.
  9th from Rev. John Warham of Dorchester.
- 225R GARLOW, MRS. EZRA CLARK, Alliance, Ohio.
  8th from Rev. Joseph Estabrook of Concord.
- 104† GAY, EBEN HOWARD, Boston. (Died February 27, 1935.)
  7th from Rev. John Cotton of Boston.
- 241* GAYLORD, MRS. EMERSON GEORGE, JR., Springfield, Pa.
  10th from Rev. Robert Gutch of Pemequid, Me.
- 181R GIBBS, MRS. CHARLES I., Brooklyn, N. Y.
  8th from Rev. Jacob Barney of Rehoboth.
- 74† GILMORE, MRS. GEORGE L., Lexington. (Died August 12, 1950.)
  8th from Rev. Samuel Whiting of Lynn.
- 11* GOODHUE, FRANCIS ABBOT, Hewlett, L. I., N. Y.
  11th from Rev. Stephen Bachiller of Lynn.
- 23* GOODHUE, MRS. FRANCIS ABBOT, Hewlett, L. I., N. Y.
  8th from Rev. John Cotton of Boston.
- 316* GOODWIN-PERKINS, CHARLES ALMON, Hoopeston, Ill.
  5th from Rev. Obadiah Borton of Evesham, N. J.
- 228 GORDON, MISS ISABEL WYMAN, Worcester.
  8th from Rev. John Sherman of Watertown.
- 194R GORDON, MRS. WILLIAM ELWOOD, Gerrardstown, W. Va.
  6th from Rev. John Vail of Woodbridge, N. J.
- 54† GREEN, MISS MARION ADELAIDE, Lancaster. (Died March 21, 1943.)
  8th from Elder William Brewster of Plymouth.
- 132† GREENE, ELBRIDGE GERRY, Lancaster. (Died July 19, 1946.)
  9th from Rev. Samuel Whiting of Lynn.
- 48† GREENE, MRS. ELBRIDGE GERRY, Lancaster. (Died August 9, 1943.)
  8th from Rev. John Cotton of Boston.
- 261 GREENE, MISS HARRIET FRANCES, Bridgton, Me.
  11th from Elder William Brewster of Plymouth.
- 288 GREENMAN, REV. LYMAN MANCHESTER, Harvard.
  10th from Rev. Stephen Bachiller of Lynn.
- 309 GRIFFITH, MISS MARGARET, San Francisco, Calif.
  6th from Rev. David Stearns of Lunenburg.

14* GUILD, GEORGE CHEEVER, Madison, Wis.
   11th from Rev. Stephen Bachiller of Lynn.
78† HALE, RICHARD WALDEN, Needham. (Died March 5, 1943.)
   5th from Rev. Nicholas Sever of Dover, N. H.
172 HALL, MRS. CHARLES P., Akron, Ohio.
   10th from Rev. Joseph Hull of Weymouth.
184* HALL, MRS. GEORGE ELMER, Hempstead, L. I., N. Y.
   6th from Rev. Ebenezer Gould of Southold, L. I., N. Y.
249* HALL, MRS. HOWARD BALDWIN, Meriden, Conn.
   7th from Rev. Samuel Stow of Middletown, Conn.
300* HAMILL, MISS MARION SUSAN, Belem, Para, Brazil.
   12th from Rev. Bachiller of Lynn.
199 HAMILTON, MRS. EDWARD PIERCE, Milton.
   10th from Rev. John Wilson of Boston.
317 HAMMON, STRATTON OWEN, Louisville, Ky.
   6th from Rev. William Hammon of Warrenton, Va.
173 HARRINGTON, ARTHUR CLARK, Leominster.
   9th from Rev. Joseph Hull of Weymouth.
162R HARRINGTON, MRS. FRENCH BATTELL, Los Angeles, Calif.
   8th from Rev. John Drake of Piscataway, N. J.
66* HARTER, MRS. FRANK EMIL, Norwalk, Ohio.
   9th from Rev. William Worcester of Salisbury.
135† HARWOOD, JOSEPH ALFRED, Lunenburg. (Died September 14, 1948.)
   9th from Elder William Brewster of Plymouth.
142* HAWTHORNE, MISS JESSICA LAUVENIA, Jericho, L. I., N. Y.
   9th from Rev. Peter Bulkeley of Concord.
204 HAY, MRS. SAMUEL, Newport News, Va.
   10th from Rev. Everardus Willemus Bogardus of New York.
318 HEATH, MRS. HOMER HARVEY, Pacific Palisades, Calif.
   7th from Rev. Michael Wigglesworth of Malden.
189* HEATHCOTE, MISS METTA, St. Petersburg, Fla.
   10th from Rev. Samuel Skelton of Salem.
188* HEATHCOTE, MRS. WILLIAM EMERSON, St. Petersburg, Fla.
   9th from Rev. Samuel Skelton of Salem.
120* HENRY, MRS. JOHN GOODRIDGE, Winchendon.
   7th from Rev. James Keith of Bridgewater.
139* HERBEN, MRS. STEPHEN JOSEPH, Maplewood, N. J.
   8th from Rev. John Sherman of Watertown.
336 HEWINS, MISS NELLIE PRISCILLA, Elmhurst, L. I., N. Y.
   9th from Rev. Samuel Skelton of Salem.
29R HODGMAN, MRS. WILLIS KENNEDY, Taunton.
   11th from Elder William Brewster of Plymouth.
130R HOLLINSHEAD, MRS. WARREN HENRY, Nashville, Tenn.
   7th from Rev. Samuel Mann of Wrentham.
220† HOLMAN, MRS. GEORGE ULYSSES GRANT, Belmont. (Died August 17, 1947.)
   8th from Rev. Samuel Mann of Wrentham.

MEMBERSHIP

218   HOLMAN, MRS. WINIFRED LOVERING, Lexington.
      10th from Rev. John Mayo of Eastham.

337   HOLTON, MISS ETHEL ELAINE, Chicago, Ill.
      8th from Rev. John Woodbridge of Andover.

304*   HOOKER, ROLAND MATHER, Miami Beach, Fla.
      10th from Rev. Richard Mather of Dorchester.

277   HOUSTON, MISS GRACE, Chicago, Ill.
      6th from Rev. James Anderson of Donegal, Pa.

335   HOUSTON, HAROLD ALLEN, Marshfield, Mo.
      6th from Rev. James Anderson of Donegal, Pa.

16†   HOWE, GEORGE ELI, Lancaster. (Died January 12, 1949.)
      10th from Rev. Stephan Bachiller of Lynn.

39*   HOWE, MRS. GEORGE ELI, Lancaster.
      7th from Rev. George Curwin of Salem.

205   HULBURT, DR. RAY GARLAND, Chicago, Ill.
      8th from Rev. Samuel Wakeman of Fairfield, Conn.

308   HULL, MRS. THOMAS NOEL, Kirksville, Mo.
      9th from Rev. Thomas Hooker of Hartford, Conn.

217R   HUTCHINS, MISS MILDRED BRIGGS, West Somerville.
      10th from Elder Thomas Cushman of Plymouth.

207R   JACKSON, RUSSELL LEIGH, Salem.
      11th from Elder William Brewster of Plymouth.

164   JOHNSON, MRS. ARTHUR MASON, Los Angeles, Calif.
      5th from Rev. Charles Peale of Chestertown, Md.

169R   JOHNSON, FREDERICK HOSMER, JR., Northborough.
      8th from Rev. Thomas Clark of Chelmsford.

171†   JOHNSON, MRS. FREDERICK HOSMER, Northborough. (Died June 16, 1950.)
      7th from Rev. Urian Oakes of Cambridge.

95*   JOHNSTON, MRS. ROBERT JAMES, Humboldt, Iowa.
      9th from Elder William Brewster of Plymouth.

263   JONES, CHARLES MARTIN, Wilmington, Del.
      10th from Rev. Henry Smith of Wethersfield, Conn.

122†   JONES, MRS. EDWARD HARTE, Chicago, Ill. (Died December 13, 1942.)
      6th from Rev. Ellis Callender of Boston.

108†   JONES, ELIOT NORRIS, Sterling. (Died February, 1948.)
      9th from Rev. Thomas Mayhew of Edgartown.

307   JONES, MRS. MILTON RAGAN, JR., Clarksdale, Miss.
      9th from Rev. Samuel Skelton of Salem.

248   JONES, REV. WILLIAM SAFFORD, D.D., Portsmouth, N. H.
      7th from Rev. Samuel Dudley of Exeter, N. H.

187   KINNAN, MISS GRACE ISABELL, Muskegon, Mich.
      9th from Rev. Everardus Willemus Bogardus of New York.

82*   KNORR, MRS. HERMANN AUGUST, Pine Bluff, Ark.
      11th from Elder William Brewster of Plymouth.

123*   LA BACH, MAJOR PAUL MAYER, Chicago, Ill.
      10th from Rev. Gideon Schaets of Albany, N. Y.

216*   LANAHAN, MRS. WILLIAM WALLACE, Towson, Md.

MEMBERSHIP

10th from Rev. William Wilkinson of King and Queen Parish, Md.

170* LANDON, HOWARD CHANDLER ROBBINS, Lancaster.
10th from Rev. John Woodbridge of Andover.

97* LANDON, MRS. WILLIAM GRINNELL, Lancaster.
9th from Rev. John Rayner of Plymouth.

230 LATHROP, ALFRED LEE, Glendale, Calif.
9th from Rev. John Lothrop of Barnstable.

271* LAWSON, MISS EDITH, New York, N. Y.
8th from Rev. Nehemiah Smith of Norwich, Conn.

89 LEPPER, MRS. EDWARD LAWRENCE, Litchfield, Conn.
8th from Rev. John Emerson of Gloucester.

223* LEOPOLD, MRS. HAROLD ELIEL, Chicago, Ill.
10th from Rev. Samuel Dudley of Exeter, N. H.

124 LEUPOLD, MRS. RICHARD JAMES, Baltimore, Md.
9th from Rev. John Gwyn of Abingdon Parish, Va.

165 LINDENBERGER, MRS. WILLIAM JAMES, San Francisco, Calif.
10th from Rev. Zachariah Symmes of Charlestown.

41† LORD, REV. AUGUSTUS MENDON, D.D., Providence, R. I. (Died September 14, 1941.)
5th from Rev. Benjamin Lord, D.D., of Norwich, Conn.

22* LORD, EDWARD CRARY, Sterling.
9th from Rev. Stephen Bachiller of Lynn.

60* LORD, MISS ELIZABETH WELLINGTON, Templeton.
9th from Rev. John Maverick of Dorchester.

149† LOWELL, ABBOTT LAWRENCE, LL.D., Ph.D, Litt.D., Boston. (Died January 6, 1943.)
9th from Rev. Francis Higginson of Salem.

133† LOWELL, MISS LUCY, Boston. (Died August 21, 1949.)
9th from Rev. Peter Bulkeley of Concord (and 36 other lines).

224 LOWELL, RALPH, Westwood.
10th from Rev. Peter Bulkeley of Concord (and 36 other lines).

87† LYNCH, MRS. JEROME MORLEY, New York, N. Y. (Died September 17, 1943.)
8th from Rev. John Warham of Dorchester.

77* MCCLEARY, MISS HELEN CARTWRIGHT, Brookline.
9th from Rev. John Eliot of Roxbury.

303 MCDONALD, HENRY TEMPLE, Harper's Ferry, W. Va.
9th from Rev. William Walton of Marblehead.

212 MACDONELL, THE HON. ALEXANDER RADCLIFFE, Savannah, Ga.
5th from Rev. Francis Pelot of Ewhaw, S. C.

33* MCGLENEN, REV. EDWARD WEBSTER, JR., North Weare, N. H.
10th from Rev. John Lothrop of Barnstable.

36* MCGLENEN, MRS. EDWARD WEBSTER, Dorchester.
9th from Rev. John Lothrop of Barnstable.

MEMBERSHIP

88† MACKENZIE, MRS. GILBERT A., Moulton, Iowa. (Died November 24, 1944.)
    5th from Rev. James Anderson of New York.
85† MCPHERSON, MRS. WILLIAM WALLACE, Chicago, Ill. (Died Nov. 25, 1945.)
    10th from Rev. John Lothrop of Barnstable.
275* MALLORY, MISS JANE HOYT, Douglaston, L. I., N. Y.
    9th from Rev. Nehemiah Smith of New London, Conn.
176† MARSHALL, MRS. FRANK, Brookline. (Died August 17, 1939.)
    9th from Rev. Peter Bulkeley of Concord.
320 MARSHALL, MRS. JULIUS DARDEN, Miami Beach, Fla.
    9th from Rev. William Wetherell of Norwell.
330* MARTIOCCIA, MRS. LIONEL JOSEPH, Daytona Beach, Fla.
    10th from Rev. John Sherman of Watertown.
158† MAY, FREDERICK GODDARD, JR., Townsend. (Died October 6, 1948.)
    8th from Rev. John Wenbourne of Manchester.
63† MAY, GEORGE HENRY, Lancaster. (Died May 25, 1945.)
    5th from Rev. Simon Huntington of Woodstock, Conn.
34* MAY, MRS. GEORGE HENRY, York, Me.
    10th from Rev. George Phillips of Watertown.
279† MAYNARD, MRS. EMMETT WEST, Newport News, Va. (Died March 25, 1945.)
    9th from Rev. Henry Jacobs of Warwisqueke Parish, Va.
155R MEIKLEJOHN, MRS. H. FRAZER, Grafton.
    10th from Rev. Stephen Bachiller of Lynn.
154R MERRIAM, MRS. PAUL ADAMS, Edgewood, R. I.
    10th from Rev. Stephen Bachiller of Lynn.
255 MESSELT, MRS. CARL TERGMAR, Gardnerville, Nevada.
    5th from Rev. John William Kurtz of Tulpehocken, Pa.
296* MILLER, ERWIN CURTIS, M.D., Worcester.
    9th from Rev. Francis Higginson of Salem.
75† MILLET, MRS. JOSIAH BYRAM, Cambridge. (Died April 24, 1941.)
    9th from Rev. John Eliot of Roxbury.
297 MILMINE, CHARLES EDWARD, Lakeville, Conn.
    11th from Rev. Ralph Partridge of Duxbury.
166* MILMINE, GEORGE PARSONS, Lakeville, Conn.
    9th from Rev. William Tompson of Braintree.
45* MILMINE, MRS. GEORGE PARSONS, Lakeville, Conn.
    10th from Rev. Ralph Partridge of Duxbury.
298 MILMINE, MISS KATHERINE, Lakeville, Conn.
    11th from Rev. Ralph Partridge of Duxbury.
147 MORRIS, LESTER DUNBAR, Peterborough, N. H.
    8th from Rev. John Wilson of Boston.
56* MORSE, MISS ESTHER CRAFTS, Lancaster.
    9th from Rev. John Lothrop of Barnstable.
210 MORSE, MRS. FRANK WILMONT, Needham.
    10th from Rev. Peter Bulkeley of Concord.

MEMBERSHIP

231 MUSGRAVE, MRS. GEORGE WILMER SAMSON, Laurel, Md.
7th from Rev. John Thomson of Bart, Pa.
302 NASH, RIGHT REVEREND NORMAN BURDETT, D.D., Boston.
8th from Rev. Samuel Stone of Hartford, Conn.
285 NEFF, LEWIS EDWIN, Tulsa, Okla.
9th from Elder William Brewster of Plymouth.
286 NEFF, WILLIAM, JR., Tulsa, Okla.
10th from Elder William Brewster of Plymouth.
294* NEWCOMBE, MRS. WILLIS EDWIN, Worcester.
8th from Rev. Jonathan Vickery of Chatham.
182* NICKERSON, MISS LOUISE ALICE, San Diego, Calif.
11th from Rev. Stephen Bachiller of Lynn.
138 NOYES, REV. MORGAN PHELPS, D.D., Montclair, N. J.
8th from Rev. James Noyes of Newbury.
322* O'BRIEN, MRS. JOHN BAYLEY, Bronxville, N. Y.
9th from Rev. Peter Hobart of Hingham.
257* OLCOTT, MISS MARY LOUISA BEATRICE, Ridgefield, Conn.
8th from Rev. John Eliot of Roxbury.
268* ORR, MRS. DUDLEY WAINWRIGHT, Concord, N. H.
8th from Rev. George Curwin of Salem.
15* PARK, REV. CHARLES EDWARDS, D.D., Boston.
9th from Rev. John Cotton of Boston.
301 PARKER, MISS CORNELIA CONWAY, Lancaster.
10th from Rev. William Walton of Marblehead.
24* PARKER, COLONEL GEORGE ALANSON, Marblehead.
10th from Rev. William Walton of Marblehead.
72 PARKER, MRS. GEORGE ALANSON, Marblehead.
10th from Rev. Joseph Hull of Weymouth.
46* PARKER, COMMANDER HARRIET FELTON, Lancaster.
10th from Rev. Ralph Partridge of Duxbury.
25* PARKER, MAJOR HAVEN, Cambridge.
9th from President Charles Chauncy of Harvard College.
40* PARKER, MRS. HAVEN, Cambridge.
11th from Rev. Stephen Bachiller of Lynn.
8† PARKER, HON. HERBERT, LL.D., Lancaster. (Died February 11, 1939.)
8th from Rev. Samuel Skelton of Salem.
12* PARKER, MRS. HERBERT, Lancaster.
9th from Rev. Ralph Partridge of Duxbury.
102* PARKER, MISS KATHERINE VOSE, Lancaster.
10th from Rev. William Walton of Marblehead.
81* PATTINSON, MRS. ISMAY GRAHAM, Pasadena, Calif.
9th from Rev. John Lothrop of Scituate.
107† PEABODY, REV. ENDICOTT, D.D., Groton. (Died November 17, 1944.)
9th from Rev. Samuel Skelton of Salem.
179 PEIRCE, CLARENCE FROST, Boston.
9th from Rev. John Miller of Groton.

MEMBERSHIP 25

38*   PEIRCE, MRS. EDWARD HENRY, Riverton, Wyoming.
         11th from Elder William Brewster of Plymouth.

161   PERCY, MRS. FREDERICK BOSWORTH, Groton.
         8th from Rev. Ralph Wheelock of Medfield.

113*   PERKINS, FRANKLIN HASKINS, M.D., Lancaster.
         8th from Rev. William Wetherell of Scituate.

118*   PERKINS, MRS. FRANKLIN HASKINS, Lancaster.
         5th from Rev. Jacobus Rutsen Hardenbergh, D.D. of Raritan, N. J.

114*   PERKINS, THE VERY REV. HOWARD DELVON, Chappaqua, N. Y.
         8th from Rev. William Wetherell of Scituate.

190R   PERRY, MRS. ARTHUR DUNTON, Barnard, Vt.
         8th from Rev. Thomas Crosby of Eastham.

58†   PIERCE, MRS. GEORGE FREDERICK, Milton. (Died October 26, 1937.)
         8th from Rev. Richard Mather of Dorchester.

151†   PIERCE, MISS CORA ELIZA, Fitchburg. (Died January 21, 1947.)
         4th from Rev. Elisha Marsh of Westminster.

229   PIERCE, REV. RICHARD DONALD, Ph.D., Boston.
         8th from Rev. Thomas Wells of Amesbury.

332   PITMAN, HAROLD MINOT, Bronxville, N. Y.
         4th from Rev. John Porter of Abington.

211†   POND, MRS. HERBERT, Keene, N. H. (Died December 6, 1948.)
         8th from Rev. John Rayner of Plymouth.

112*   POND, THOMAS TEMPLE, Boston.
         8th from Rev. Samuel Man of Wrentham.

276*   POOR, MRS. CLARENCE HENRY, JR., Cambridge.
         8th from Rev. Thomas Carter of Woburn.

185R   PORTER, MISS MARY GURLEY, Castine, Me.
         8th from Rev. Robert Jordon of Spurwink, Me.

10*   POTTER, MRS. MURRAY ANTHONY, Lancaster.
         9th from Rev. Thomas Walley of Barnstable.

273   REED, EDWARD VERNON, Methuen.
         10th from Rev. John Lothrop of Scituate.

115*   ROBBINS, THE VERY REV. HOWARD CHANDLER, D.D., Heath.
         9th from Rev. John Rayner of Plymouth.

203   ROBINS, ARTHUR DE BERDT, South Orange, N. J.
         4th from Rt. Rev. William White, D.D., of Philadelphia, Pa.

69†   RUSSELL, HARRY BROWNING, Dartmouth. (Died December 15, 1934.)
         10th from Rev. Stephen Bachiller of Lynn.

221*   SALTONSTALL, HON. LEVERETT, LL.D., Chestnut Hill.
         11th from Rev. Francis Higginson of Salem.

238   SANGER, MISS MARY ELIZABETH, South Braintree.
         12th from Rev. Stephen Bachiller of Lynn.

239*   SAPP, MRS. FREDERICK ARTHUR, Ottawa, Ill.
         9th from Rev. Samuel Skelton of Salem.

MEMBERSHIP

235* SCOTT, MISS HARRIETT GRACE, Brookline.
9th from Rev. Joseph Hull of Weymouth.

202* SEYMOUR, PRESIDENT CHARLES, Ph.D., Litt.D., LL.D., Yale University.
8th from Rev. John Woodbridge of Andover.

310* SHEA, MISS LOREA CHILTON, Worcester.
13th from Rev. Robert Peck of Hingham.

252† SHORT, MRS. THOMAS FRANCIS, Du Queen, Ark. (Died August 15, 1944.)
4th from Rev. John Cameron, D.D., of St. James' Parish, Va.

178* SIDENER, REV. HERMAN SUKER, S.T.D., Canton, Ohio.
11th from Rev. John Lothrop of Scituate.

110R SILLIMAN, REV. VINCENT BROWN, Hollis, N. Y.
8th from Rev. John Jones of Concord.

148R SIMMONS, FREDERICK JOHNSON, Keene, N. H.
9th from Rev. Thomas Tupper of Sandwich.

246 SMALL, CARLETON POTTER, Portland, Me.
10th from Rev. John Cotton of Boston.

251 SMALL, MRS. RICHARD DEERING, Portland, Me.
9th from Rev. John Cotton of Boston.

103* SNOW, DONALD KENNEDY, Chicago, Ill.
10th from Elder William Brewster of Plymouth.

30† SNOW, REV. SYDNEY BRUCE, D.D., Ph.D., Chicago, Ill. (Died April 7, 1944.)
9th from Elder William Brewster of Plymouth.

152† SPARKS, MRS. EDWIN ERLE, Riverton, N. J. (Died February 27, 1943.)
8th from Rev. Peter Hobart of Hingham.

168† SPRAGUE, MRS. HENRY HARRISON, Boston. (Died 1937.)
3rd from Rev. Ephraim Ward of West Brookfield.

175R SPURR, MRS. WILLIAM FESSENDEN, Dorchester.
6th from Rev. John Peirce of Swansea.

293 SQUIRE, ROBERT ALLEN, Meriden, Conn.
9th from Rev. John Warham of Dorchester.

208* STAINES, MISS PHILA LINVILLE, Allendale, N. J.
11th from Rev. Thomas Carter of Woburn.

43* STAINES, SAMUEL EDGAR, Allendale, N. J.
10th from Rev. Thomas Carter of Woburn.

226† STEVENS, RT. REV. W. BERTRAND, D.D., LL.D., Los Angeles, Calif. (Died August 22, 1947.)
9th from Rev. Thomas Millet of Gloucester.

242* STONE, MRS. BENJAMIN JOHNSON, Byfield.
10th from Rev. Robert Gutch of Pemequid, Me.

156R STONE, ROGER POMEROY, Hingham.
11th from Elder William Brewster of Plymouth.

35* STONEHAM, MRS. ELBRIDGE FERNALD, Exeter, N. H.
9th from Rev. William Tompson of Braintree.

49* STOREY, MRS. RICHARD CUTTS, JR., Hamilton.
9th from Rev. Nathaniel Ward of Ipswich.

MEMBERSHIP

289 STRIDER, MRS. CLIFFORD ROYCE, Guthrie, Okla.
    10th from Rev. John Warham of Dorchester.
292* STUART, HAROLD LEONARD, Chicago, Ill.
    9th from Rev. Roger Williams of Providence, R. I.
291* STUART, MISS HARRIET FRANCES BARNES, Chicago, Ill.
    9th from Rev. Roger Williams of Providence, R. I.
206 SUMMERALL, GENERAL CHARLES PELOT, LL.D., D.Mil.Sc., Charleston, S. C.
    4th from Rev. Francis Pelot of Ewhaw, S. C.
254R TALIAFERRO, MRS. CHARLES CHAMPE, 2nd., Wilmington, Del.
    5th from Rev. John William Kurtz of Tulpehocken, Pa.
287 TAYLOR, ALDRICH, Lancaster.
    7th from Rev. John Avery of Truro.
198† TEDCASTLE, MRS. ARTHUR WHITE, Rome, Ga. (Died May 11, 1942.)
    5th from Rev. Francis Pelot of Ewhaw, S. C.
281 TELFORD, MRS. WORTHINGTON SMITH, Sarasota, Fla.
    4th from Rev. Job Swift, D.D., of Richmond.
183 TER HEUN, MRS. DEWITT, New York, N. Y.
    11th from Elder William Brewster of Plymouth.
19† THAYER, MRS. BAYARD, Lancaster. (Died March 31, 1941.)
    8th from Rev. John Mayo of Barnstable.
26* THAYER, MAJOR DUNCAN FORBES, Lancaster.
    9th from Rev. Nathaniel Ward of Ipswich.
111* THAYER, MRS. DUNCAN FORBES, Lancaster.
    10th from Rev. John Wilson of Elizabeth River Parish, Va.
6†   THAYER, COLONEL JOHN ELIOT, Lancaster. (Died July 22, 1933.)
    7th from Rev. John Cotton of Boston.
7†   THAYER, MRS. JOHN ELIOT, Lancaster. (Died October 23, 1943.)
    7th from President Charles Chauncy of Cambridge.
28* THAYER, HON. JOHN ELIOT, JR., Milton.
    9th from Rev. Nathaniel Ward of Ipswich.
37† THAYER, MRS. NATHANIEL, Lancaster. (Died September 29, 1934.)
    10th from Rev. Stephen Bachiller of Lynn.
174 THOMPSON, RALPH NEWELL, Pittsburgh, Pa.
    9th from Rev. William Tompson of Braintree.
62* TOUSLEY, BENNETT EDWIN, Philadelphia, Pa.
    9th from Rev. John Lothrop of Barnstable.
136† TUTTLE, MRS. GEORGE FULLER, Scarsdale, N. Y. (Died January 22, 1938.)
    9th from Rev. George Phillips of Watertown.
180† VON SCHWINBECK, MRS. JOSEPH CARL, St. Louis, Mo. (Died December 31, 1949.)
    9th from Rev. Stephen Bachiller of Lynn.
264 VOSE, FREDERIC PERRY, Evanston, Ill.
    9th from Rev. Ralph Partridge of Duxbury.

274 WALES, MISS MARION PORTER, Chicago, Ill.
    10th from Rev. Peter Bulkeley of Concord.
260* WALKER, MRS. FREDERICK, South Portland, Me.
    3rd from Rev. John Strickland, Jr., of Oakham.
245 WANDS, MRS. IRA BURTON, Los Angeles, Calif.
    9th from Rev. Hawte Wyatt of Jamestown, Va.
163 WARD, MRS. CHARLES CRESAP, South Pasadena, Calif.
    8th from Rev. Anthony Jacob Henckel of Germantown, Pa.
278* WEINMANN, MRS. JOHN FRANCIS, Little Rock, Ark.
    9th from Rev. John Lyford of Plymouth.
282† WEIS, MISS ANNA LORA, Athens, Vt. (Died January 21, 1950.)
    9th from Rev. Stephen Bachiller of Lynn.
1* WEIS, REV. FREDERICK LEWIS, Th.D., Lancaster.
    10th from Rev. Stephen Bachiller of Lynn.
2* WEIS, MRS. FREDERICK LEWIS, Lancaster.
    11th from Elder William Brewster of Plymouth.
283† WEIS, JOHN PETER CARL, Lincoln, R. I. (Died December 31, 1945.)
    9th from Rev. Stephen Bachiller of Lynn.
98* WEIS, ROBERT POMEROY, Lancaster.
    12th from Elder William Brewster of Plymouth.
177 WEISNER, MRS. B. J., Salisbury, N. C.
    11th from Rev. Stephen Bachiller of Lynn.
134† WESTCOTT, MRS. ARTHUR CLEMENT, Allentown, Pa. (Died May 14, 1942.)
    9th from Rev. John Mayo of Eastham.
232R WESTGATE, MRS. CLIFFORD EARLE, Tacoma, Wash.
    9th from Rev. Henry Dunster of Harvard College.
327* WETTSTEIN, JOHN CARPENTER, Williston Park, N. Y.
    13th from Rev. Robert Peck of Hingham.
31* WHEELWRIGHT, GEORGE WILLIAM, III, Lancaster.
    9th from Rev. John Wheelwright of Salisbury.
32* WHEELWRIGHT, MRS. GEORGE WILLIAM, Lancaster.
    5th from Rev. William Balch of Bradford.
91* WHITE, MRS. MICHAEL MORGAN, Paris, France.
    11th from Rev. Peter Bulkeley of Concord.
329* WHITEHILL, WALTER MUIR, Ph.D., North Andover.
    7th from Rev. Israel Loring of Sudbury.
215* WILDER, MRS. EDWARD FRANKLIN, South Hingham.
    9th from Rev. Samuel Stone of Hartford, Conn.
311* WILER, MRS. ALFRED HENRY, JR., Miami Beach, Fla.
    11th from Rev. Henry Smith of Wethersfield, Conn.
144 WILLIAMS, LIEUTENANT LESTER JAMES, M.D., Baton Rouge, La.
    8th from Rev. Thomas Buckingham of Saybrook, Conn.
20* WILSON, REV. JOHN HENRY, Wilton, N. H.
    11th from Elder William Brewster of Plymouth.

328	WOLFE, MRS. JAMES WATSON, Chicago, Ill.
	5th from Rev. Joseph Willard of Mendon.
321	WOLFRAM, REV. GERTRUDE METLEN, Zarephath, N. J.
	6th from Rev. Jacob Godschalk of Germantown, Pa.
323	WOODS, MISS LOTTIE GERTRUDE, San Francisco, Calif.
	8th from Rev. Samuel Dudley of Exeter, N. H.
125R	WORRALL, MRS. BYRON K., Lincoln, Neb.
	10th from Rev. Ralph Wheelock of Medfield.
334	WRIGHT, DANIEL WENTWORTH, Basking Ridge, N. J.
	6th from Rev. John Norton of East Hampton, Conn.
143†	WRIGHT, HOWARD HARLAN PAIGE, Winchester. (Died January 11, 1947.)
	9th from Rev. John Lothrop of Scituate.
64*	WRIGHT, MRS. HOWARD HARLAN PAIGE, Winchester.
	11th from Rev. Stephen Bachiller of Lynn.
259*	WRIGHT, REV. WILLIAM RECORD, South Berwick, Me.
	4th from Rev. John Strickland, Jr., of Oakham.
338	WYATT, MRS. JOHN WILLIAM, Danville, Va.
	8th from Rev. Antonius Jacob Henckel of Germantown, Pa.
59*	YEAGER, MRS. MILBURN EDGAR, Needham.
	8th from Rev. John Wheelwright of Salisbury.

MEMBERSHIP

1950

Life Members, 1950	141
Annual Members, 1950	106
Active Membership, 1950	247

Active Membership, 1950	247
Resignations, 1933-1950	26
Deaths, 1933-1950	61
Total Membership, 1950	334

1933-1950

Total Life Members	176
Total Annual Members	158
Total Membership	334
Life Members Died	35
Annual Members Died	26
Annual Members Resigned	26
Died or Resigned	87

* Life Members.
R Resigned or Dropped.
† Deceased.

THE COLONIAL CLERGY OF MARYLAND, 1629-1776

ALEXANDER ADAMS (See *C.C.Del.*), sett. Somerset Parish, Md., 1704-1769; Stepney Parish, 1704-1769; Ep.; d. Stepney Parish, Md., 1769.

ALEXANDER ADAMS, JR., son of the Rev. Alexander Adams, Ord. London, lic. Dec. 21, 1748, K.B. Md., Jan. 24, 1748/9; sett. St. James' Parish at Herring Creek (Anne Arundel) Md., 1748-1767; Ep., d. St. James' Parish, Md., Oct. 20, 1767.

HENRY ADDISON, A.M., b. St. John's Parish (Prince George) Md., 1717, son of Thomas Addison; Queen's Coll., Oxford, matric., Mar. 3, 1734/5, ae. 16, A.B., 1738, A.M., 1741; Ord. England, 1742; sett. Piscataway Parish, St. John's Chh. at Broad Creek, Md., 1742-1789; Tory; Ep., d. St. John's Parish, Md., 1789, ae. 72.

THOMAS AIREY, b. Kendal, Yorks., England, 1701; K.B. Md. Jan. 24, 1725/6; sett. Great Choptank Parish (Dorchester) Md., at Cambridge, 1727-1765; Ep.

BENNETT ALLEN, A.M., b. Hereford, Eng., 1737, son of Rev. James Allen of Yazor, Hereford, England; matric. Wadham Coll., Oxford, Mar. 27, 1754, ae. 17; A.B., 1757, A.M.; Ord. (Bsp. Oxford), Sept. 20, 1761, lic. Sept. 30, 1766, K.B. Md., Oct. 2, 1766; sett. Annapolis (Anne Arundel) Md., St. Anne's Chh., 1767-1768; All Saints' Parish (Frederick) Md., May 27, 1768-1777; returned to England, 1777; killed Lloyd Dulany in a duel, June 18, 1782; Ep., d. England, after 1782.

PATRICK ALLISON, D.D., b. Lancaster Co., Pa., 1740, son of William and Catharine (Craig) Allison; A.B., U. of Pa., 1760, A.M., D.D., 1782; Tutor, 1762-1763; Prof. at Newark Academy, Del., 1761-1763; Ord. Philadelphia, Pa., 1765; sett. Baltimore, Md., 1763-1802; Chaplain, Congress, 1776; a founder of Baltimore College and Baltimore Library; in 1763, Baltimore contained 30-40 houses and some 300 inhabitants; Presb.; d. Baltimore, Md., Aug. 24, 1802, ae. 62 (GS).

JOHN ALTHAM (alias Gravenor), came from England in the "Ark & Dove" with Lord Baltimore to Maryland, Mar. 25, 1634; sett. St. Mary's City (St. Mary's) Md., Mar. 1634-1639; Kent Island (Queen Annes), 1639-1640; S.J., R.C.; d. St. Mary's City, Md., Nov. 5, 1640.

JOHN ANDREWS, D.D. (See *C.C.Del.*), sett. as Rector, St. John's Parish (Caroline) Md., 1772-1776; Rector, York, Pa., St. John's Chh., 1776-1782; Rector, St. Thomas' Parish (Balt.), Md., Apr. 13, 1782-1785; Ep.; d. Philadelphia, Pa., Mar. 29, 1813, ae. 67.

RICHARD ARCHBOLD, arriv. Md., 1740; S.J., R.C.

BISHOP FRANCIS ASBURY, b. Handsworth, near Birmingham, England, Aug. 20, 1745, son of Joseph and Elizabeth Asbury; lic. London, Aug. 18, 1767; English ministry: Bedfordshire circuit, 1767; Colchester circuit, 1768; Northamptonshire, 1769; Hampshire, 1770; arriv. at Philadelphia, Sept. 27, 1771; Am. ministry: New York and vicinity, 1771-1772; appointed Supt. of missionary work in Am., Oct. 10, 1772; sett. at Baltimore, Md., July 14, 1773-1778; New Mills, Pemberton, N. J., 1775; miss. to Md., Va. and N. C., 1778-1784; Ord. Bishop, Dec. 25, 1784-1816; Meth.; d. Spottsylvania, Va., Mar. 31, 1816, ae. 74 yrs.

JAMES ASHBEY, sett. Bohemia (Cecil) Md., St. Xavier's Chh., 1705-1746; Newtown (St. Mary's) Md., St. Francis Xavier's Chh., 1767; R.C.; d. Newtown, Md., 1767.

JOHN ASHTON, sett. Doughoregan (Howard) Md.; Baltimore, Md., St. Peter's Chh., 1756; S.J., R.C.

THOMAS ATKIN, lic. Feb. 25, 1766; K.B. Md., Mar. 3, 1766; Curate, St. John's Parish (Caroline) Md., 1766-1767; Ep.

PETER ATTWOOD, came to Md., 1711; sett. Charles Co., 1711-1731; in St. Mary's Co., 1732-1734; Superior, 1728, 1733; S.J.; R.C.; d. Newtown, Md., Dec. 25, 1734.

THOMAS BACON, b. Isle of Man, England, ca. 1700, brother of Sir Anthony Bacon; custom's official, Dublin, Ireland, 1736-1737; Ord. Kirk Michael, Mar. 10, 1744/5; Chaplain to Lord Baltimore, 1745; sett. St. Peter's Parish (Talbot) Md., 1745-1757; sett. Oxford (Talbot), Md., 1745-1757; All Saints' Parish (Frederick) Md., 1758-1768; Ep., d. All Saints' Parish, Md., May 24, 1768.

JOHN GEORGE BAGER, b. Niederlinzweiler, Nassau-Saarbruch, Mar. 29, 1725, son of a Lutheran minister; Univ. of Halle; sett. Simmern, Palatinate; arriv. Philadelphia, Pa., Oct. 23, 1752; sett. Baltimore, Md., 1755-1762; sett. Hanover (York) Pa., St. Michael's Chh., Nov. 10, 1752-1763, 1769-1791; West Manheim, Pa., St. David's or Sherman's Chh., 1753-1790; sett. New York City, Trinity Chh., 1762-1767, and Old Swamp Chh., 1763-1767; Lower Windsor (York) Pa., 1767-1769; West Manchester, Pa., St. Paul's or Wolf's Chh., 1767-1769; York, Pa., Christ Chh., 1767-1769; Chambersburg (Franklin) Pa., 1767-1769; Guilford, Pa. (Grindstone Hill Chh.) 1767-1770; Berwick (Adams) Pa., 1768-1791; Hopewell (York) Pa., Blimyers Chh., 1767-1791; Hellam, Pa., Kreutz Creek Chh., 1768-1791; Windsor, Pa., Emanuel or Frysville Chh., 1771-1776; Luth.; d. Hanover, Pa., June 9, 1791.

DESOLATE BAKER, see Henry Loveall.

HEZEKIAH BALCH, D.D., b. Deer Creek (Harford) Md., 1741, A.B., Princeton, 1766, A.M., 1774, D.D., Williams, 1806; taught school in Fauquier Co., Va.; lic. May 17, 1769; Ord. Va., Mar. 8, 1770; sett. Bethel, S. C., 1770-1774; Bethesda, S. C., 1770-1774; installed, Emmitsburg, Md., Oct. 16, 1775-1778; York, Pa., 1775-1776; Greenville, Tenn., 1785-1800; Pres. and founder, Greenville Coll., Tenn., 1794-1810; Presb.; d. Greenville, Tenn., Apr. 1810.

JOHN BARCLAY, A.M., b. Windsor, Eng., Mar. 28, 1732, son of Rev. James Barclay, Canon of Windsor; matric., King's Coll., Cambridge, 1750, from Eaton, A.B., 1755, A.M., 1758, Fellow, 1753; sett. Cumberland Parish (Lunenburg) Va., 1756-1757; Oxford, Md., 1758-1770; St. Peter's Parish (Talbot) Md., 1758-1770; Ep.

WILLIAM BARROLL, A.B., b. Herefordshire, England, 1734, son of William and Abigail (Jones) Barroll; A.B., St. John's Coll., Cambridge, 1757; Ord. London, Sept. 23, 1759; lic. Mar. 4, 1760; K.B. Md., Mar. 18, 1760; sett. North Sassafras Parish (Cecil) Md., St. Stephen's Chh., 1760-1776; resided at Elkton, Md., 1776; nephew of Rev. Hugh Jones, whom he succeeded; Ep.; d. Elkton, Md., 1778, ae. ca. 40.

ANDREW BAY, b. Ireland; Ord. New Castle Presbytery, 1748; sett. Hopewell (York) Pa., Shrewsbury Chh., Round Hill, 1747-1760; Highland (Adams) Pa., Lower Marsh Creek Chh., 1747-1760; Churchville (Harford) Md., Deer Creek Chh., 1760-1768; supply, Bethel, Md., 1764-1767; Albany, N. Y., 1768-1773; Newtown, L. I., N. Y., 1773-Apr. 1775, resigned; New Side Presb.; d. 1777.

THOMAS BAYLEY (possibly b. 1687, son of William Bayley of Marlborough, Wilts., Eng.; matric. Brasenose, Oxford, Feb. 17, 1701/2, ae. 15; A.B., 1705); K.B. Narragansett, Mar. 27, 1712; sett. Baltimore, Md., St. John's Chh., 1713-1723; itin. min., N. C.; sett. Newport Parish (Isle of Wight) Va., 1724; Lynnhaven Parish (Princess Anne) Va., 1728; returned to Eng., 1729; Ep.

JAMES BEADNALL, b. Northumberland, England, Apr. 8, 1718; adm. S.J. at Walten, Sept. 7, 1739; sett. Newtown (St. Mary's), Md., St. Francis Xavier's Chh., 1749-1772; Chapel Point (Charles) Md., St. Ignatius' Chh., at St. Thomas' Manor, 1749-1772; arrested in Md., Sept. 22, 1756; R.C.; d. Newtown, Md., Sept. 1, 1772.

FRANCIS BEAUMONT, alias Williams, came to Md., 1711; returned to England, 1716; S.J., R.C.

WILLIAM BECKINGHAM, b. England; bapt. ca. Jan. 28, 1697, as a Quaker Baptist; sett. Newtown, Upper Providence, Pa., Oct. 12, 1697-1701; sett. Nottingham, Md., 1700-1701; was living in Chester Co., Pa., 1680, 1688, at Chichester, Feb. 14, 1701; mason; bought house and 150 acres of land at Upper Providence, Apr. 7, 1687, and on Oct. 1, 1696, another 100 acres; 7th Day Bapt.; d. Chester Co., Pa., ca. 1701.

HAMILTON BELL, educated at the Log College, 1738; lic. by Philadelphia Presbytery, Sept. 30, 1740; Ord. East Donegal, Pa., Nov. 11, 1742-1745; became an Episcopalian; Ord. London, 1747; lic. Oct. 19, 1747; K.B. Md., Oct. 27, 1747; sett. Somerset Parish (Somerset) Md., Chhs. at Princess Anne and Monie, 1748-1783; St. Mary Anne's Parish (Cecil) Md., 1767-1773; Presb.-Ep.; d. Somerset Parish, Md., 1783.

HAMILTON BELL, JR., A.B., b. Somerset Co., Md., 1740, son of Rev. Hamilton Bell; A.B., U. of Pa., 1769; Ord. 1774; sett. Stepney

Parish (Wicomico) Md., 1777-1786; Somerset Parish, Md., 1786-1794; Ep.; d. Somerset Parish, Md., 1794 ae. 54.

JOHN BENNETT, alias Gosling, arriv. 1723; at Annapolis, Md., 1723-1729; returned to England, 1729; S.J., R.C.; d. England, Apr. 13, 1751.

JEREMIAH BERRY, b. St. John's Parish (Prince George) Md., Ord. 1768; lic. for Md., Dec. 22, 1768; K.B., Md., Jan. 19, 1769; sett. All Saints' Parish (Frederick) Md., at Monocacy, 1769-1783; Ep., d. after 1783.

PAUL BERTRAND, K.B. Md., 1685; sett. William and Mary Parish (St. Mary's) Md., 1689-1691; St. Mary's City, Md., St. George's Chh., Poplar Hill, 1689-1691; Ep.

JOHN BOARMAN, arr. Md., Mar. 21, 1774; R.C.; d. Newtown, 1794.

SYLVESTER BOARMAN, arr. Md. Mar. 21, 1774; R.C.

FRANCIS BOEHLER, brother of Bishop John Peter Boehler, arriv. in Am., May 17, 1752; Ord. after 1752; in charge of the School at Salisbury, Pa., Jan. 1755; sett. Graceham, Md., 1762-1764; Hope, N. J., 1773; Kingsbury, N. Y., 1773-1777; Emaus, Salisbury, Pa., 1777-1779; Moravian; d. Lititz, Pa., 1806.

JOHN BOLTON, came to Md., S.J., R.C.

JOHN BOONE, arr. Md., 1765; R.C.; d. St. Inigoes, Apr. 11, 1795.

STEPHEN BORDLEY, son of Rev. Stephen Bordley, of St. Paul's, London; induct. St. Paul's Parish (Kent) Md., July 2, 1697-1709; Shrewsbury Parish (Cecil), Md., Apr. 6, 1702-1707; Ep.; d. St. Paul's Parish, Md., Aug. 25, 1709.

JONATHAN BOUCHER, A.M., b. Blencogo, Cumberland, England, Mar. 12, 1737/8, son of James and Ann (Barnes) Boucher; educated at St. Bees, Eng., A.M. (Hon.) Columbia, 1771; D.D.; arriv. Urbana, Va., July 12, 1759; taught school at Port Royal, Va., res. Mt. Church, Essex Co.; St. Mary's Parish (Caroline) Va., 1759-1762; Ord. by Bsp. of London, Mar. 26, 1762; K.B. Va., Mar. 30, 1762; sett. St. Mary's Parish (Caroline) Va., 1763-1770; Hanover Parish (King George) Va., 1762-1770; Annapolis, Md., St. Anne's Chh., 1770-1775; inst. Queen Anne's Parish (Prince George) Md., St. Barnabas's Chh., Aug. 14, 1772-1775; loyalist, returned to Eng., Sept. 1775; sett. Epsom, Surrey, Eng., 1784-1799; sett. Carlisle, Eng., 1799-1804; Ep.; d. Carlisle, Cumberland, Eng., Apr. 27, 1804.

RICHARD BOUCHER, priest in Md.; R.C.; d. England, 1760.

WILLIAM BOUCHER, R.C. priest in Md.; d. England, Sept. 28, 1757.

BENEDICT BOURDILLON, Ord. 1735; sett. Somerset Parish, Md., 1735-1739; Baltimore, Md., St. Paul's Chh., July 24, 1739-1745; Ep. of Huguenot origin; d. Baltimore, Md., Jan. 5, 1745.

JOHN BOWIE, D.D., b. Prince George Co., Md., 1747; Ord. London, 1771; lic. July 28, 1771; curate, Prince George Parish (Montgomery) Md., 1771-1772; sett. Worcester Parish, Md., St. Martin's Chh. at Berlin, 1772-1775; St. Peter's Parish (Talbot), Md., 1775-1785; Oxford, Md., 1775-1785; Great Choptank Parish, Md., 1785-1790; Rector, St. Michael's Parish, Md., 1790-1801; imprisoned, 1777; Ep.; d. St. Michael's, Md., 1802.

JOHN BRADFORD (poss. b. Athy, 1710, son of Alexander Bradford, gent., pens. Trinity Coll., Dublin, Oct. 27, 1727, ae. 17, A.B., 1732, A.M., 1735); sett. North Elk Parish (Cecil) Md., St. Mary Anne's Chh., Nov. 20, 1744-1745; Ep.; d. North Elk Parish, Md., Mar. 22, 1744/5.

THOMAS BRATTON, educ. U. of Glasgow; came to Md., 1711; sett. Manokin Chh., Princess Anne, Md., 1711-1712; Wicomico Chh., Salisbury, Md., 1711-1712; Presb.; d. Eastern Shore, Md., Oct. 1712.

JAMES BRECHIN, K.B. Md., Dec. 10, 1695 (as Breechin); sett. All Hallow's Parish (Worcester) Md., 1696-1698; Coventry Parish (Somerset) Md., 1696-1698; K.B. Va., Nov. 16, 1702; sett. Cople Parish (Westmoreland) Va., 1702-1714; St. Paul's Parish (Hanover) Va., 1704-1705; liv. in Va., 1719; Ep.

CHARLES BROCKHOLES, Md., 1711-1716; returned to England, 1716; S.J., R.C.

WILLIAM BROGDON, son of William Brogdon of Calvert Co., Md.; prob. pens. Trinity Coll., Dublin, July 26, 1727; K.B. Va., Sept. 11, 1735; Ord. Westminster, Aug. 6, 1735; sett. All Hallow's Parish (Anne Arundel) Md., 1735-1751; Dorchester Parish (Dorchester) Md., 1736-1739; Queen Anne's Parish (Prince George) Md., 1751-1770; Ep.; d. Queen Anne's Parish, Md., 1770.

SAMUEL BROOK (See *C.C.Del.*), sett. St. George's Parish (Harford) Md., 1754; Ep.; d. New Castle, Del., Oct. 25, 1756.

CLEMENT BROOKE, b. Prince George Co., Md., ca. 1730; K.B. S.C., Feb. 7, 1775; sett. Annapolis, Md., St. Anne's Chh., 1756-1759; Prince George Parish (Montgomery) Md., 1759-1761; St. Andrew's Parish (St. Mary's) Md., 1761-1762; to Va. from Md., 1762; sett. Overwharton Parish (Stafford) Va. 1764-1776; member Committee of Safety, Stafford Co., Va.; Ep.; d. Prince George Co., Md., 1800, ae. ca. 70 years.

MATTHEW BROOKE, arriv. Md., 1702; S.J., R.C.; d. St. Thomas' Manor, Md., 1702.

ROBERT BROOKE, b. Md., 1663; S.J. at Walten, 1684; sett. Port Tobacco, Md., St. Ignatius' Chh. 1697-1714; Newport, Md., Jesuit Chapel, 1697-1714; Zekiah Swamp Creek, Md., Boarman Estate, 1697-1714; first native R.C. priest in Md.; Superior, Jesuit Order, 1710-1714; R.C.; d. Newtown (Charles) Md., July 18, 1714.

DINAH BROWN, chosen minister at Brick Meeting House, East Nottingham (Cecil) Md., Jan. 17, 1735/6; Friend.

JAMES BROWN (brother of Willian Brown, Sen.), arr. N. Y. C., 1686; sett. Marcus Hook (Chester) Pa.; sett. East Nottingham, Md.; Friends' minister; d. Nottingham, Md., 1715.

JOSHUA BROWN, minister at Brick Meeting House; visited Nantucket, Mass., 1770; Friend.

RICHARD BROWN, M.D., b. Trinity Parish (Charles) Md., ca. 1724; educ. in Scotland; Ord. 1750; lic. July 9, 1750; K.B. Md., July 18, 1750; sett. King and Queen Parish, Md., 1747-1773; res. 1773; physician; Ep., d. Trinity Parish, Md., 1789, ae. 65.

THOMAS BROWN, A.B., b. Holywell, Oxford, England, 1731, son of Thomas Brown; matric. Magdalen Hall, May 20, 1748, ae. 17; A.B., St. Alban's Hall, Oxford, Jan. 17, 1752; Chaplain, 27th Regt., at Albany, N. Y., 1754-1764; Ord. London, July 8, 1764; K.B. Aug. 20, 1764; sett. Albany, N. Y., St. Peter's Chh., 1764-1768; Schenectady, N. Y., St. George's Chh., 1764-1768; Dorchester Parish, Md., 1768-induct. May 30, 1772-1782; St. Luke's Parish (Queen Annes) Md., 1782-1784; Ep; d. Dorchester, Md., May 2, 1784, ae. 54.

WILLIAM BROWN, b. 1655, son of William Browne of Puddington, Notts., England; came to Am., 1682; sett. Marcus Hook, Pa.; removed to Nottingham Lots (Cecil) Md., 1702; minister at the Brick m. h., East Nottingham; Friend; d. East Nottingham, Md., June 23, 1746, ae. 91 yrs.

WILLIAM BROWN, JR., son of James and Honor (Clayton) Brown; chosen minister, Brick m. h., East Nottingham, Jan. 17, 1735/6; visited many Friends' meetings in Am. and in Europe, 1750-1754.

JOHN CONRAD BUCHER, b. Neunkirch, Schaffhausen, Switzerland, June 13, 1730, son of Landvogt Johann Jacob and Anna Dorothea (Burgauer) Bucher; matric. U. of Marbourg, July 14, 1752; U. of Basel; arriv. in Am., 1755; Ord. ca. June 20, 1767; sett. Carlisle (Cumb.) Pa. 1762-1768; Elizabeth (Lanc.) Pa., White Oaks Chh., 1763-1769; Elizabethtown, Pa., 1763-1779; Pittsburgh, Pa., Chh. at Fort Pitt, 1764-1766; Sharpsburg (Allegheny) Pa., 1764-1766; Shippensburg (Cumb.) Pa., 1764-1766; (also Bedford and Coxtown, Pa., 1764-1766); Conococheague, Md., St. Paul's Chh., 1765-1768; Middletown (Fredk.) Md., Zion or Kittatinny Mountain Chh., 1765-1768; Derry (Dauphin) Pa., Hummelstown Chh., 1765-1769; Lebanon (Leb.) Pa., Tabor Chh., 1767-Nov. 24, 1768-July 7, 1780; Chambersburg (Frank.) Pa., Falling Spring Chh., 1767-1778; East Donegal (Lanc.) Pa., Maytown Chh., 1767-1779; Mt. Joy, Pa., Miller's Chh., 1767-1779; Reading (Berks) Pa., 1769-1770; Manheim (Lanc.) Pa., St. Paul's Chh., 1771-1778; Rapho, Pa., 1771-1778; Warwick, Pa., Kissel Hill Chh., 1771-1778; North Annville (Leb.) Pa., Hill Chh. or Quittopehilla Chh., 1771-1778; Jonestown, Pa., 1771-1778; Swatara, Pa., Little Swatara Chh., 1771-1778; Pa. Troops, Lieut., Apr. 19, 1760-1764; Capt., July 31, 1764-1765; comm. Ensign, 1st Battal. Pa., Regt., Apr. 11, 1758; Chaplain, Rev., 1775-Aug. 1, 1777; German Reformed; d. Annville, Pa., Aug. 15, 1780.

THE COLONIAL CLERGY OF MARYLAND 37

THOMAS BUDD, sett. Newtown, Upper Providence, Pa., Oct. 12, 1697-1701; Nottingham, Md., ca. 1701; 7th Day Bapt.

JOHN BURNYEAT, Quaker preacher in Md., 1665, at Patuxent, 1671, and West River, 1672; Friend.

EDWARD BUTLER, Ord. for Va. Feb. 1704/5; K.B., Va., Feb. 3, 1704/5; in Va. 1705; sett. Durham Parish (Charles) Md., Chh. at Nanjemoy, 1710-1711; Port Tobacco Parish, Md., 1710-1711; Annapolis, Md., St. Anne's Chh., Mar. 7, 1712/3-Nov. 9, 1713; Ep.; d. Annapolis, Md., Nov. 9. 1713.

ISAAC CAMPBELL, b. Scotland, ca. 1724; Ord. 1747; lic. for Va., July 6, 1747; K.B. Va., July 13, 1747; sett. Trinity Parish (Charles) Md., letter of induction, June 11, 1751-1784; Ep.; d. Trinity Parish, Md., July 30, 1784, ae. ca. 60 yrs.

DAVID CANDLER, sett. Frederick (Fredk.), Md., 1743-1744; Monocacy Chh., Md., 1743-1744; York, Pa., 1743-1744; Hanover (York) Pa., St. Michael's Chh., 1743-1744; (also Conowago (Adams) Pa. 1743-1744) his parish extended from the Susquehanna to the Potomac; Luth.; d. Hanover, Pa., Dec., 1744.

HENRY CAREW, sett. Newport, Md., 1677-1683; Superior, 1677; President of the Franciscan missions, 1677; R.C.; d. at sea on way back to England, 1683.

HUGH CARLISLE, sett. St. George's Parish (Harford) Md., 1744-1749; Ep.

JAMES CARROLL, arr. Md., 1749; R.C.; d. Newtown Manor, 1756.

ARCHBISHOP JOHN CARROLL, b. Upper Marlborough, Md., Jan. 8, 1735, son of Daniel and Eleanor (Darnall) Carroll; educ. at St. Omer's Coll., Flanders; adm. S.J., 1753; stud. phil. and theol. at Liege and St. Omer's, 1755; Ord. priest, 1769; taught phil. and theol. at St. Omer's and Liege, 1769-1773; return. to Md., June 26, 1774; missionary to Md. and Va., 1774; Superior of Missions, U. S. A., June 6, 1754; sett. Baltimore, Md., 1774-1775, 1786-1787; trustee, St. John's Coll., Annapolis; fdr. Georgetown Coll., 1791; Prest. Trustees, Baltimore Coll., 1803; app. Bishop, U. S. A., Nov. 6, 1789; consecrated, Aug. 15, 1790; archbshp., 1808; R.C.; d. Baltimore, Md., Dec. 3, 1815.

JAMES CASE, arriv. Md., 1724; S.J., R.C.; d. St. Inigoes, Md., Feb. 15, 1731.

HENRY CATTAWAY, arriv. Md., 1703; S.J., R.C.; returned to England, 1706.

JONATHAN CAY (or Kay), b. Northumberland, Eng.; K.B. Md., Aug. 16, 1711; sett. William and Mary Parish (Charles) Md., 1712-1715; sett. Christ Chh. Parish (Calvert) Md., Jan 27, 1714/5-1730; Ep.

WALTER CHALMERS, sett. Westminster Parish (Anne Arundel) Md., ca. 1753; Ep.

SAMUEL CHASE, sett. Port Tobacco Parish (Charles) Md., 1742-1742; Ep.; d. or returned to Eng., 1742.

THOMAS CHASE, lic. Feb. 12, 1738/9; K.B. Md., Feb. 21, 1738/9; sett. Somerset Co., Md., 1739-1743; Baltimore, Md., St. Paul's Chh., (1739)-1743-1775; "his son Samuel Chase, a signer of the Dec. of Indep., was b. Somerset Co., Md., 1741"; Ep.

JOHN CHURCHMAN, b. June 4, 1705, son of John and Hannah (Cerie) Churchman; chosen minister at Brick m. h., East Nottingham (Cecil) Md., Jan. 17, 1735/6; visited Friends in Newbury and Nantucket, Mass., 1742; with his brother-in-law, William Brown, visited Friends meetings in Europe, 1750-1754.

SAMUEL CLAGGETT, son of Richard Claggett, Ord. London, Dec. 20, 1747; Rector, Christ Chh. Parish (Calvert) Md., at Port Republic, 1747-(1767); Rector, William and Mary Parish (Charles), Md.; Ep.; d. William and Mary Parish, Md.

BISHOP THOMAS JOHN CLAGGETT, D.D., b. Prince George Co., Md., Oct. 2, 1743, son of Rev. Samuel and Elizabeth (Gantt) Claggett; A.B., Princeton, 1764, A.M.; D.D., Princeton, 1787; D.D., Washington Coll., Md.; Ord. London, Oct. 11, 1767; K.B. Md., Oct. 23, 1767; sett. as curate, Annapolis, Md., St. Anne's Chh., 1767-1768; All Saints' Parish (Calvert) Md., 1768-1776; Christ Chh. Parish, Md., 1768-1775; St. Paul's (Pr. Geo.) Md., 1779-1781; Queen Caroline (Ann Arundel) Md., 1781-1782; St. Paul's, Md., 1782-1786, 1792, 1810; St. James's Parish (Ann Arundel) Md., 1786-1792; Trinity Parish, Upper Marlborough, Md., 1810-1816; Bsp. of Md., Sept. 13, 1792-1816; Chaplain, U. S. Senate, 1800; Ep.; d. Upper Marlborough, Md., Aug. 2, 1816, ae. 73.

JOHN CLARKE, A.B., b. 1718, A.B., Princeton, 1759; lic. 1759; Ord. 1760; inst. Upper Mount Bethel (Northampton) Pa., Forks North Chh., Oct. 13, 1762-Nov. 4, 1767; sett. Allen, Pa., 1762-1767; sett. Bethel (Harford) Md., 1769-1781; sett. Bethel and Lebanon, Pa., 1781-1797; Presb.; d. Western Penna., 1797.

Father CLAVERING, S.J., R.C., in Md. 1674.

THOMAS CLAYLAND, had been a Presb. or Cong.; sett. St. Michael's Parish (Talbot) Md., 1672-(1692?); St. Peter's Parish, Md., 1694-1696; (a *John* Clayland is noted, 1697-1715; Presb.-Ep.).

JOHN CLEMENT, b. Great Britain; Ord. Rehoboth (Somerset) Md., June, 1719-1720; sett. Gloucester (Camden) N. J., Timber Creek Chh., at Blackwood, 1720-(1750?); Pilesgrove, N. J., 1720-1720-(1741?); Presb.; d. 1766.

JOSIAH COALE, Quaker preacher in Md., 1660, for ten weeks; had been expelled from Va. and N. E.; returned to Eng.; Friend.

THOMAS COCKSHUTE (Cockshutt), sett. All Saints' Parish (Calvert) Md., 1697-1720; signed a letter as minister, June 29, 1720; Ep.

JOSEPH COLEBATCH (Colbatch), A.B., b. Derbyshire, England; matric., St. Edmund's Hall, Oxford, Dec. 15, 1690; A.B., Oriel

Coll., 1694; Ord. London, July 4, 1694; K.B. Md., Jan. 11, 1697/8; sett. All Hallow's Parish (Anne Arundel) Md., South River, 1694-1734; Ep.; d. All Hallow's Parish, Md., Jan. 1734.

PEREGRINE CONEY, B.D., A.B., Emmanuel Coll., Cambridge, 1677, A.M., 1681, Fellow; B.D. Oxford, 1688; Rector, North Luffenham, Rutland, Eng., 1690; came to Md. 1694; sett. Annapolis, Md., St. Anne's Chh., 1696-1704; William and Mary Parish (St. Mary's) Md., 1696-1698; St. Mary's City, Md., St. George' Chh., Poplar Hill, 1696-1698; Chaplain to Gov. Nicholson, 1704; Ep.

HUGH CONN, A.B., b. Macgilligan, Ireland, ca. 1685; U. of Glasgow; came from London, 1714; sett. Mount Paran (Baltimore) Md., at North Point, 1714-1715, first services held in Baltimore Co.; Ord. Patapsco, Md., Oct. 1715-Sept. 1719; Baldensburg (Prince George) Md., East Branch of the Potomac and Pomonkey, 1719-1752; Presb.; b. Bladensburg, Md., June 28, 1752.

JOHN COOPER, b. Hampshire, England, arriv. Md., 1644; sett. St. Mary's City, Md., 1644-1646; R.C.; d. Va., 1646.

ROBERT COOPER, D.D., b. Northern Ireland, ca. 1732; A.B., Princeton, 1763; D.D., Dickinson Coll., 1792; Ord. Southampton (Cumberland) Pa., Middle Spring Chh., Nov. 21, 1765-Apr. 12, 1797; West Nottingham (Chester) Pa., 1765-1797; Lower West Nottingham (Cecil) Md., 1765-1797; Captain, Pa. Volunteers, 1776; Trustee Dickinson Coll., 1783-1805; Presb.; d. Shippensburg, Middle Spring, Pa., Apr. 5, 1805, ae. 72.

THOMAS COPLEY (alias Philip Fisher), b. Madrid, 1595/6, son of William Copley of Gatton, England; arriv. Md., Aug. 8, 1637; sett. St. Mary's City (St. Mary's) Md., 1637-1645, 1648-1653; taken in chains to England, 1645; released, 1648; arriv. Va., Jan. 1648; Superior, Jesuit Order, 1642-1645, 1648-1653; R.C.; d. Patapsco, Md., 1653.

JAMES COX; sett. Charles City Co., Va., 1723-(1729?); St. Paul's Parish, (Queen Annes) Md., 1729-1753; St. John's Parish (Caroline) Md., 1748-1753; Ep.; d. St. Paul's Parish, Md., 1753.

THOMAS CRADOCK, b. Wolversham, Bedfordshire, Eng., 1718; educ. at Cambridge; lic. Feb. 21, 1743/4; K.G. Md., Feb. 28, 1743/4; sett. St. Thomas' Parish (Baltimore) Md., St. Thomas Chh., Owings Mills, Garrison Forest, Feb. 4, 1744/5-1770; brother of John Cradock, Archbishop of Dublin, 1772-1777; Ep.; d. St. Thomas' Parish, Md., May 7, 1770, ae. 51.

JAMES CRAWFORD, K.B. Md., Jan. 8, 1711/2; sett. William and Mary Parish (St. Mary's) Md., 1694-1696; St. Mary's City, Md., 1694-1696; evidently ret. to England, and then in 1712, to Md.; Ep.

RALPH CROUCH, sett. St. Mary's City, Md., 1657-1657; R.C.

ENOCH DAVID, b. Duck Creek, Del., Feb. 22, 1718; called to the ministry at Welsh Tract, 1751; became a Sabbatarian, 1752; Ord. Oct. 16, 1769; sett. Nottingham, Md., 1769-1772; Newtown, Pa., 1769-1772; Lower Dublin, Pa., 1769-1772; Warwick (Chester)

Pa., French Creek Chh. at East Nantmeal, 1769-1770; only 7th Day Bapt. minister in Pa., 1770.

JOHN DAVIS, b. Upper Dublin, Pa., Sept. 10, 1721; Ord. Montgomery, Pa., 1756: sett. Winter Run (Harford) Md., 1754-1809; Harford (Harford) Md., Harford Bapt. Chh., 1754-1809; Baltimore, Md., 1769-1775; Bapt.; d. Winter Run, Md., 1809, ae. 87 yrs.

PETER DAVIS, in Md., 1721-1734; S.J., R.C.; d. England, July 1, 1759.

SAMUEL DAVIS (See *C.C.Del.*), sett. Snow Hill, Md., 1686-1698, 1718-1725; Presb.; d. Snow Hill, Md., 1725.

THOMAS DAVIS, Came to Md., 1691; sett. King and Queen Parish (St. Mary's), Md., 1691-1696; St. Mary's City, Md., 1692-1694; William and Mary Parish, 1692-1694; All Faith's Parish (St. Mary's) Md., 1694-1695; St. Paul's Parish (Prince George) Md., 1694-1695; St. George's Parish (Harford) Md., 1694-1695; Ep.

HUGH DEANE, sett. St. John's or Copley Parish (Baltimore) Md., Sept. 24, 1739-1776; Ep.

LAURENCE DeBUTTS, b. Sligo, Ireland, 1693, son of John DeButts, merchant, pens. Trinity Coll., Dublin, June 23, 1711, ae. 18; K.B. Va., July 9, 1721; sett. Washington Parish (Westmoreland) Va., 1721-1728; St. Stephen's Parish (Northumberland) Va., 1723-1726; St. Mary's Parish (Culpeper) Va., 1731-1733; Truro Parish (Fairfax) Va., Pohick Chh., 1733-1734; St. Mary's City, Md., St. George's Chh., Poplar Hill, 1735-1752; William and Mary Parish (St. Mary's) Md., 1735-1752; St. Andrew's Parish (St. Mary's) Md., at Leonardstown, 1744-1753; All Faiths' Parish (St. Mary's) Md., 1744-(1734)-1763; (and poss. Trinity Parish (Charles) Md., 1744-1763); Ep.; d. Md., 1763.

GABRIEL D'EMILHANE, K.B. Md., Mar. 7, 1700/1; Port Tobacco Parish (Charles), 1702-1703; also preached in Calvert Co., Md., 1703; Ep.

JOHN BAPTISTE De RITTER, arr. Md., 1765; sett. Goshenhoppen, Pa., 1774; R.C.; d. Oct. 3, 1786.

BERNARD DIDERICK, b. Belgium; sett. Conowago (Adams) Pa., Sacred Heart Chh., 1758-1758; Deer Creek (Harford) Md., St. Joseph's Chapel, 1775-1776; Baltimore, Md., St. Peter's Chh., 1775-1782; R.C.; d. Sept. 1793.

JOHN DIGGES, JR., sett. Deer Creek (Harford) Md., St. Joseph's Chapel, 1742-1747; R.C.; d. Nov. 1761.

THOMAS DIGGES, arr. Md., 1742; at Sequanock, 1753; R.C.

JOHN DONALDSON, b. Scotland; K.B. Md., Feb. 12, 1711/2; induct. Somerset Parish (Somerset) Md., 1712-1715; Westminster Parish (Anne Arundel) Md., time not stated; King and Queen Parish (St. Mary's) Md., 1715-1747; Ep.; d. King and Queen Parish, Md., 1747.

WILLIAM DONALDSON, Ord. Pa., 1755; sett. Waccamaw,

S. C., at Conwaysboro, Horry District, ca., 1752, 1756; Snow Hill (Worcester) Md., ca. 1755; Presb.

WILLIAM DOWIE, lic. Apr. 2, 1762; K.B. Md., Apr. 6, 1762; sett. Durham Parish (Charles) Md., at Nanjemoy, 1762-1767; Ep.

WILLIAM DUKE, b. Patapsco Neck, Baltimore Co., Md., Sept. 15, 1757; itinerant Methodist minister in Frederick Co., Md., 1774-1780; became an Episcopalian; Rector, Queen Caroline Parish, Elk Ridge (Howard) Md., 1780, 1785-1786; sett. Lancaster, Pa., 1781; Ord. (Ep.), Oct. 1785; sett. St. Paul's Parish (Prince George) Md., 1787-1791; North Elk Parish, Md., 1792-1796; Rector, St. Margaret's, Westminster, Md., 1796-1799; Annapolis, Md., St. Anne's Chh., 1803-1806; Meth.-Ep.; d. 1840.

JEREMIAH EATON, sett. St. George's Parish (Harford) Md., 1675-(1683); Ep.

NICHOLAS HENRY EBERHARD, b. Jan. 2, 1723; arriv. Bethlehem, Pa., Dec. 10, 1751; sett. Warwick (Lanc.) Pa., St. James's Chh. at Lititz, 1765-1767; Graceham (Frederick) Md., 1767-1770; Moravian; d. Graceham, Md., Apr. 8, 1770.

SAMUEL EDGAR, sett. Annapolis, Md., St. Anne's Chh., Jan. 29, 1743/4-1744; Ep.

WILLIAM EDMISTON, A.M., son of William and Mary Edmiston; A.B., U. of Pa., 1759, A.M.; lic. as a Preb.; Ord. England (Epis.); lic. Mar. 30, 1767; K.B. Md., Mar. 31, 1767; sett. St. James's Parish (Anne Arundel) Md., at Herring Creek, 1767-1768; Annapolis, Md., St. Anne's Chh., June 12, 1768-Jan. 1770; St. George's Parish (Harford) Md., 1770-1772; St. Thomas' Parish (Baltimore) Md., at Garrison Forest, 1770-1775; left during the Am. Rev.; Presb.-Ep.

JOHN EDWARDS (possibly b. 1678, son of Thomas Edwards of Llanwrthwl, Co. Brecon; matric. Merton Coll., Oxford, Feb. 21, 1694/5, ae. 17; A.B., Mar. 9, 1698/9), K.B. Md., May 7, 1701; sett. St. John's Parish (Balt.) Md., 1702-1711; and prob. also sett. at St. George's Parish (Harford) Md., 1702-1711; Ep.

ESDRAS THEODORE EDZARD, sett. Hanover Parish (King George) Va., 1727; Westminster Parish (Anne Arundel) Md., 1730-1730; gave up the ministry and kept a tavern at Falmouth, Va., 1757-1763; Ep.; d. Falmouth, Va., 1763.

RICHARD ELLIS, arr. Md., 1749; R.C.

EVAN EVANS, D.D., b. Carnoe, Montgomery, Wales, 1671, son of Evan David Evans, matric. St. Alban's Hall, Oxford, Mar. 12, 1691/2, ae. 21 yrs; A.B., Brasnose Coll., Oxford, 1695, A.M., 1714, B.D., 1714, D.D., 1714; Ord. London, 1700; K.B., Pa., July 5, 1700; K.B. Philadelphia, Aug. 9, 1708; sett. Philadelphia, Pa., Christ Church, 1700-Feb. 15, 1717/8, res.; Lower Providence (Mont.) Pa., St. James's Chh. at Evansburg, 1700-1707, 1709-1716; Newtown (Del.) Pa., St. David's Chh. at Radnor, 1700-1714, 1716-1718; Concord, Pa., St. John's Chh., 1700-1703; Chester, Pa., St. Paul's Chh., 1702-1704; Oxford (Chester) Pa., Trinity Chh., 1716-1718; (also preached in Welsh at Montgomery, 1700-1704 and Radnor; and at Chichester, 1700-1704, Oxford, 1702-1704, Perkiomen, Newcastle, 1700-1705 all in Pa. and Evesham, N. J., 1700-1713); sett. St. George's Parish (Harford) Md., Spesutia Chh. near Perrymans, 1718-1721; Ep.; d. St. George's Parish, Md., Oct. 1721.

JOHN EVERSFIELD (D.D.?), b. Tunbridge, Kent, England, 1703, son of Matthew Eversfield; matric. St. Mary's Hall, Oxford, Apr. 6, 1723, ae. 20; A.B., Feb. 14, 1726/7; Ord. London, Sept. 25, 1727; lic. Sept. 25, 1727; K.B. Md., Sept. 26, 1727; sett. St. Paul's Parish (Prince George) Md., May 1728-1780; Ep.; d. St. Paul's Parish, Md., Nov., 8, 1780, ae. ca. 80.

JOHN CHRISTOPHER FABER, b. Mosbach on the Neckar, Rhein-Pfaltz, 1732, son of a minister at Gimmeldingen, and cousin of Rev. John Theobald Faber; matric. Heidelberg, Feb. 26, 1752; arriv. Philadelphia, 1767, having been ordained in Germany; sett. Worcester (Montgomery) Pa., Wentz's Chh., Skippack, Oct. 1767-Oct. 1768; Baltimore, Md., 1st Germ. Ref. Chh., 1768-1771; Pipe Creek, Md., 1768-1775; Taneytown, Md., 1772-1785; West Manheim, Pa., David's or Sherman's Chh., 1772-1776; Codorus (York) Pa., St. Jacob's Chh., 1776-1776; also Zion's Chh., Blimyer's Chh. and Jerusalem Chh., all in Pa., 1776; German Reformed; d. 1796.

RALPH FALKNER, arr. Md., 1762; R.C.

JAMES FARRAR, arriv. Md., 1733; sett. Anne Arundel Co., Md., 1737-1738; Newtown, 1742; S.J., R.C.; d. Hooton, Cheshire, England, July 18, 1753.

HENRY FENDALL, sett. Durham Parish, Md., 1775-1775; Ep.

JAMES FINLEY (or Findley), b. Co. Armagh, Ireland, Feb. 1725; educated by Rev. Samuel Blair; Ord. East Nottingham (Cecil) Md., Rock Chh., 1752-May 17, 1782, dism.; Elk, Md., 1760-1782; Rehoboth and Round Hill Chhs. at Forks of the Youghiogheny, western Pa., 1783-1795; Justice of the the Peace and Judge of Common Pleas, 1783; Presb.; d. Forks of the Youghiogheny, Pa., Jan. 6, 1795.

SAMUEL FINLEY, D.D., b. Co. Armagh, Ireland, 1715; arriv. Philadelphia, Sept. 28, 1734; attended the Log Coll., D.D. (Hon) Princeton, 1749, D.D. U. Glasgow, 1763; lic. Aug. 5, 1740; Ord. as an evangelist at New Brunswick, N. J., Oct. 13, 1742; sett. Deerfield, Greenwich and Cape May, N. J., 1740-1743; Lower West Nottingham, Md., June 14, 1744-1761; West Nottingham (Chester) Pa., 1744-1761; Princeton, N. J., 1761-1766; president of Princeton Univ., July, 1761-1766; Presb.; d. Philadelphia, Pa., July 17, 1766, ae. ca. 60 (GS).

PHILIP FISHER, see Thomas Copley.

FRANCIS FITZHERBERT, arriv. Md., 1654; sett. St. Mary's City, Md., 1654-1660; St. Inigoes, Md., Chh. of the Assumption, 1654-1660; was arraigned, 1657; S.J., R.C.

Father FITZWILLIAMS, alias Villiers, S.J., R.C.; d. Md., 1665.

JOHN FLEETWOOD, arriv. Md., 1734; S.J., R.C.; d. Newtown, Md., Jan. 5, 1734/5.

THOMAS FLETCHER (poss. b. Chibour, Kent, 1690, son of Thomas Fletcher, gent.; matric. Univ. Coll., Oxford, Apr. 2, 1707, ae. 17; A.B., Dec. 18, 1710—as Wm. Fletcher); K.B. Md., July 9, 1721; sett. All Hallows' Parish (Worcester) Md., 1721-1740; Ep.

FRANCIS FLOYD, arriv. Md., 1724; S.J., R.C.; d. Newtown Manor, Md., Nov. 13, 1729.

GEORGE WILLIAM FORESTER (a William Forster, b. 1722, son of Joseph Forster of Newton, Northumberland, armiger, matric. Lincoln Coll., Oxford, Mar. 19, 1740/1, ae. 18 yrs., A.B., 1744); induct. Shrewsbury Parish (Kent) Md., Aug. 6, 1745-1774; Wye Mills (Talbot) Md., St. Luke's Chh., 1745-1774; Ep.; d. Shrewsbury Parish, Md., Nov. 12, 1774.

MICHAEL FORSTER (alias Gulick), see Michael Gulick.

GEORGE FOX, b. Fenny Drayton, Leicestershire, England, July, 1724, son of Christopher Fox; founder of the Society of Friends, 1669; preached in Scotland, 1657, Ireland, 1669, Jamaica, West Indies and the British Colonies in North America, Maryland, Penna., etc., 1671-1672, Holland, 1677, and 1684, was imprisoned at Scarborough, Eng., 1663-1666 and at Worcester, England, 1673-1674; Friend (or Quaker); d. Jan. 13, 1691.

JAMES AUGUSTIN FRAMBACK, arr. Md., 1758; R.C.; d. St. Inigoes, Md., Apr. 17, 1795.

THEODORE FRANKENFIELD, b. Herborn, Germany, Nov. 25, 1727, son of Nicholas Herbert Frankenfield; educ. Herborn, Apr. 26, 1736-Apr. 27, 1741; Ord. The Hague, 1762; arriv. N. Y. C., July 27, 1752, and at Frederick, Md., May 4, 1753; sett. Frederick, Md., 1753-1756; Monocacy Chh., Frederick, Md., 1753-1756; Conococheague, Md., 1753-1756; Union (Adams) Pa., 1753-1756; Conowago, Pa., 1753-1756, Zion's or Quickel's Chh., German Reformed; d. Frederick, Md., June, 1756.

JOHN FRASER, b. Scotland; Ord. Aug. 29, 1700; sett. Hood, Co. Durham, England, 1697-1699; K.B. Va. Sept. 18, 1700; arriv. Nov. 1, 1701; sett. Overwharton Parish (Stafford) Va., 1702-1705; St. Paul's Parish (King George) Va., 1702-1705; Durham Parish (Charles) Md., 1705-1710; Port Tobacco Parish, Md., 1705-1710; induct. Piscataway Parish (Prince George) Md., Mar. 15, 1709/10; Piscataway Parish (Prince George) Md., 1710-1742; Ep.; d. Piscataway Parish, Md., Nov. 1742.

DANIEL FRISTOE, b. Chappawomsick, Stafford Co., Va., Dec. 7, 1739, brother of William Fristoe; Ord. June 15, 1771; sett. Old Seneca (Montgomery) Md., Bapt. Chh., 1773-1774; Brenttown (Fauquier) Va., 1774-1774; Bapt.; d. Marcus Hook, Pa., 1774, ae. 35.

ANNE (WEBB) GALLOWAY, dau. of Borrington Webb, of London, England; a recognized preacher of the Society of Friends at West River, Md., as early as 1679; m. in 1689, Samuel Galloway, b.

1659; d. West River, Md., 1720; she died at West River, Md., 1722.

EDWARD GANTT, M.D., b. Prince George Co., Md., ca. 1741; A.B., Princeton, 1762; M.D., Edinburgh; Ord. England, 1770; K.B. Md., Feb. 20, 1770; sett. Somerset Parish, Md., as curate, 1770-1771; Piscataway Parish, Md., curate, 1770-1775; All Hallows' Parish (Worcester) Md., Jan. 1775-1780; Queen Anne's Parish (Prince George) Md., 1780-1795; Georgetown, D. C.; sett. Ky., 1808; physician; chaplain, U. S. Senate, 1801-1804; Ep., became a Swedenborgian; d. near Louisville, Ky., 1837, ae. 96.

FREEBORN GARRETTSON, b. Md., Aug. 15, 1752; sett. Frederick Co., Md., 1776-1776; N. Y. Conference, 1776-1827; Meth.; d. N. E., Sept. 26, 1827, ae. 45.

PHILIP GATCH (See *C.C.Del.*), sett. Frederick Co., Md., 1774-1774; Meth.; d. Clermont Co., Ohio, Dec. 25, 1835.

THOMAS GAVAN, came to Md., 1677; sett. Md., 1677-1685; Superior, 1677; S.J., R.C.; returned to England, 1685.

ANDREW GEDDES, sett. All Saints' Parish (Calvert) Md., 1696; lay reader; Ep.

THOMAS GERARD, arriv. Md., 1734; S.J., R.C.; d. England, 1761.

WILLIAM GERARD, arriv. 1719; S.J., R.C.; d. St. Inigoes, Md., Apr. 16, 1731.

JOHN SIEGFRIED GEROCK, A.M., b. Wuertemburg; Ord. Darmstadt, Hessen, before 1752; arriv. Charleston, S. C., 1753; sett. Lancaster, Pa., Holy Trinity Chh., Mar. 1753-Mar. 29, 1767; Strasburg, Pa., St. Michael's or Beaver Creek Chh., 1753-1767; Sharpsburg (Worcester) Md., 1758-1767; N. Y., N. Y., Holy Trinity Chh., 1769-1773; Baltimore, Md., 1773-1787; Luth., d. Baltimore, Md., 1787.

PATRICK GLASCOW (or Glasgow), sett. Rehoboth (Somerset) Md., Pocomoke Chh. (1st Presb. in Am.), 1735-1741; Ord. Princess Anne, Md., New Side Presb. Chh., 1736-1741; became an Epis.; Ord. (Epis.), ca. 1741; sett. All Hallows' Parish (Worcester) Md., 1741-1753; Worcester Parish (Worc.) Md., 1744-1753; Presb.-Ep.; d. All Hallows' Parish, Md., Mar. 23, 1753.

GEORGE GOLDIE, b. England, 1741; lic. for Va., Feb. 25, 1766; Ord. 1766; K.B. Va., Mar. 3, 1766; sett. All Saints' Parish (Frederick) Md., 1767-1772; King and Queen Parish (St. Mary's) Md., 1772-1791; Rector, Hanover Parish (King George) Va., 1779-1780; Ep.; d. King and Queen Parish, Md., 1791, ae. 50.

JOHN GORDON, D.D., b. Aberdeen, Scotland, 1717, son of Dr. John Gordon; matric. Queen's Coll., Oxford, July 14, 1737, ae. 20; Ord. 1745; sett. Annapolis, Md., St. Anne's Chh., Apr. 22, 1745-1749; St. Michael's Parish (Talbot) Md., at St. Michael's, 1750-1790; Ep.; d. St. Michael's, Md., 1790, ae. 70.

MATTHEW GOTTLIEB GOTTSCHALK, b. Arnswalde, Brandenburg, Germany, 1716; theol. student at Lindheim, 1744, ae.

28 yrs.; sett. Antietam, Md., 1745-1747; Conococheague, Md., 1745-1747; Monocacy, Md., 1745-1747; South Branch of the Potomac, West Va., 1745-1747; sett. Bethlehem, Pa., 1747-1748 as an itinerant minister in Pa. at Alsace, Coventry, Goshenhoppen, Neshaminy, Oley and Skippack, 1747-1748; Moravian; d. Bethlehem, Pa., Aug. 1748.

GEORGE GOWNDREL, app. priest to Md., Mar. 31, 1770; K.B. Md., Apr. 3, 1770; sett. St. Andrew's Parish (St. Mary's) Md., 1773-1775; Ep.

JOHN GRAVENOR, see John Altham.

JOSEPH GREATON, sett. Md., 1721-1732; Sacred Heart Chh., Conewago, Pa., 1721-1752; St. Joseph's Chh., Philadelphia, Pa., 1733-1750; Superior, 1745; S.J., R.C.; d. Bohemia Manor, Aug. 19, 1753.

GEORGE ADAM GUETING, sett. Antietam, Md., 1772-1804; Germ. Reform.

MICHAEL GULICK (alias Forster), opened a Catholic College in Md., 1677; Superior, Jesuit Order; R.C.; d. Feb. 6, 1684.

NICHOLAS GULICK, arriv. Md., 1675; sett. St. Mary's City, Md., 1675-1697; St. Inigoes (St. Mary's) Md., 1697; Newtown, Md., St. Francis Xavier's Chh., 1697; S.J.; R.C.

WALTER HACKETT (See *C.C.Del.*), sett. North Elk Parish (Cecil) Md., St. Mary Anne's Chh., 1733-1735; Ep.; d. North Elk Parish, Md., 1735.

JAMES HADDOCK, came to Md., 1699; S.J., R.C.

JOHN VALENTINE HAIDT, arriv. N. Y. C., Apr. 15, 1754; sett. Philadelphia, Pa., 1754-1756; Graceham, Md., 1757-1758; Bethlehem, Pa., 1758-1780; painter; Moravian; d. Bethlehem, Pa., Jan. 1780.

HENRY HALL, K.B. Va., Jan. 11, 1697/8; sett. All Saints' Parish (Calvert) Md., 1684-1695; Christ Church Parish (Calvert) Md., 1695-1697; St. James's Parish (Anne Arundel) Md., at Herring Creek, 1695-inducted May 7, 1698-1721; Ep.

JOHN HALL, sett. St. Mary's Co., as follows: St. Mary's City, Md., 1697-1704; St. Inigoes, 1697; Newtown, 1697; R.C.; d. Ghent, July 9, 1703.

RICHARD HALL (prob. b. Yorkshire, 1658, son of Charles Hall, pens. Trinity Coll., Dublin, Apr. 3, 1676, ae. 18 yrs.; A.B., 1681, A.M., 1684); sett. Christ Church Parish (Calvert) Md., 1694-1694; Ep.

JOHN HAMILTON, A.B., b. Strabane, Tyrone Co., Ireland, 1706, son of Claude Hamilton, gent., pens. Trinity Coll., Dublin, Apr. 14, 1725, ae. 19, A.B., 1733; sett. North Elk Parish (Cecil) Md., St. Mary Anne's Chh., Dec. 10, 1745-inducted Apr. 4, 1746-1773; St. Mary Anne's Parish (Cecil) Md., 1753, and prob. 1745-1767; Ep.; d. North Elk Parish, Md., Apr. 12, 1773.

JOHN HAMILTON (or Hambleton), Ord. Rehoboth, Md., 1746; sett. Rehoboth (Somerset) Md., Pocomoke Chh., 1746-1756;

Princess Anne, Md., Manokin Chh., 1746-1756; Salisbury (Charles) Md., Wicomico Chh., 1746-1756; Chestertown (Kent) Md., 1750-1756; Old Side Presb.; d. 1756.

JOHN HAMPTON, b. Scotland, arriv. Am., 1705; Ord. Snow Hill (Worc.) Md., Mar. 1707-1718; Pitts Creek (Som.) Md., 1709-1717; Rehoboth, Md., Pocomoke Chh., 1717-1722; 1st Presb. minister to be ordained in Am.; will proved, Feb. 2, 1721(/2); d. Snow Hill, Md., Jan. 1721/2.

WILLIAM HANNA, A.M., b. Litchfield, Conn., ca. 1738; A.B., Columbia, 1759, A.M., 1765, A.M., Yale, 1768; Ord. Albany, N. Y. (Presb.), 1761-May 1767; became an Ep.; Ord. (Ep.) by Bsp. of London, 1772; lic. for Culpeper Co. Va., June 11, 1772; K.B. Va., June 18, 1772; Culpeper Co. Va., 1772-1775; sett. Christ Church Parish (Queen Annes) Md., 1775; Westminster Parish, Md., 1778-1785; Annapolis, Md., St. Anne's Chh., 1779-1780; attorney and physician; Presb.-Ep.; d. Westminster Parish (Anne Arundel) Md., 1785, ae. 48.

ROBERT HARDING, sett. St. Thomas' Manor, Md., 1732-1749; St. Joseph's Chh., Philadelphia, Pa., 1749-1772; Sacred Heart Chh., Conewago, Pa., 1749-1772; St. Mary's Chh., Phila., 1763-1772; S.J., R.C.

ELIZABETH HARRIS, Quaker missionary at Severn River and Kent Island, Md., Sept. 1656; returned to England before Jan. 14, 1657/8; Friend.

JOHN HARRIS, A.B. (See *C.C.Del.*), sett. Princess Anne (Somerset) Md., Manokin Chh., 1756-1764; Salisbury (Charles) Md., Wicomico Chh., 1756-1764; Presb.; d. 1790.

MATHIAS HARRIS, sett. Chester Parish (Kent) Md., as curate, June 10, 1766-1773; inducted Chester Parish, Mar. 14, 1773-Aug. 5, 1773; Ep.

HENRY HARRISON, alias John Smith, sett., N.Y.C., asst., 1683-1687; in Ireland, etc., 1687-1697; in Md., 1697-1701; S.J., R.C.; d. Md., 1701.

WALTER HANSON HARRISON, b. Durham Parish (Charles) Md., ca. 1748; Ord. 1774; K.B. Md., Nov. 16, 1774; sett. St. Paul's Parish (Prince George) Md., as curate, 1774-1776; Queen Anne's Parish, Md., 1776-1779; Durham Parish, Md., 1779-1798; Ep.; d. Durham Parish, Md., 1798, ae. ca. 50.

BERNARD HARTWELL, sett. St. Mary's City, Md., 1645-1646; Superior for six months; R.C.; d. St. Inigoes, Md., 1646.

RICHARD HARTWELL, A.B., b. Hamilton's Banne, Co. Armagh, Ireland, 1706, son of Richard Hartswell, gent., pens, Trinity Coll., Dublin, July 9, 1724, a. 18; A.B., 1729; sett. Bristol Parish (Dinwiddie) Va., 1739; Prince George Parish (Montgomery) Md., 1749-1751; Ep.

JOHN CHRISTOPHER HARTWIG, b. Thueringen, Saxe Gotha, Germany, Jan. 6, 1714; Ord. London, England, Nov. 24,

1745; sett. Bedminster (Somerset) N. J., St. Paul's Chh., 1745-1748; New Germantown, N. J., Zion's Chh. at Tewksbury, 1745-1748 (also at Raritan and Huntingdon Co.); East Camp, N. Y., Christ Church, 1746-1760; Hackensack, N. J., 1748-1749; Mahwah (Bergen) N. J., Ramapo Chh., 1748-1749; New York, N. Y., Holy Trinity Chh., 1748-1749, 1761, 1782; Saddle River (Bergen) N. J., Zion Chh., 1748-1749; Rhinebeck (Dutchess) N. Y., 1749-1750, and nearby places; Wurtenbergh, N. Y., 1749-1750; Upper Providence (Montgomery) Pa., Augustus Chh. at Trappe, 1751-1751; Goshehoppen, Pa., 1751; Exeter (Berks) Pa., Schwartzwald Chh., 1757-1759; Muhlenberg, Pa., Alsace Chh., 1757-1759; Reading, Pa., Trinity Chh., 1757-1759; Frederick, Md., 1762, 1768-1769; Winchester, Va., 1762, 1769, 1781; Boston, Mass., 1784; Waldoboro, Me.; Chaplain of a German regt. in the French and Indian War; left his large estate to found Hartwig Seminary at Hartwig, Otsego Co. N. Y., 1816; Lutheran; d. Claremont, N. Y., July 17, 1796, ae. 82.

THOMAS HARVEY, arriv. N. Y. C., Aug. 1683; sett. New York, N. Y., Oct. 30, 1683-1688, also Jesuit chaplain for Gov. Col. Thomas Dongan of N. Y.; went to Md., 1688; sett. St. Mary's City, Md., 1688-1696; assumed name Smith occasionally to escape the penal code; R.C.; d. St. Mary's City, Md., 1696, ae. 84.

JOSEPH HATTERSTY, arr. America, July 12, 1762; sett. Newtown, Md., 1769; R.C.; d. Philadelphia, Pa., May 8, 1770, ae. 35.

BERNARD MICHAEL HAUSIL, b. Heilbronn, Wuertemberg, 1727, son of Rev. Bernard Hausil; arriv. Annapolis, Md., 1752; Ord. Luth.; sett. Frederick, Md., 1752-1759; Antietam, Md., 1754-1759; Berks Co. Pa., as follows: Exeter, Muhlenberg and Reading, 1759-1762, and Perry, Zion's Chh., 1759-1763; Easton (Northampton) Pa., St. John's Chh., 1763-1769; Upper Saucon (Lehigh) Pa., St. Paul's, Blue or Organ Chh., 1764-1769; Elizabethtown (Lanc.) Pa., Christ Chh., 1766-1768; New York, N. Y., Holy Trinity, 1770-1783, senior minister; Tory; became an Ep.; Ord. by Bsp. of London, 1785; sett. St. George's Parish, Halifax, Nova Scotia, 1795-1799; Luth.-Ep.; d. Halifax, N. S., Mar. 9, 1799.

THOMAS HAVERS, S.J., R.C., sett. Md., 1704-1709.

TIMOTHY HAYES, alias Hanmer, S.J., R.C.; sett. Md., 1634-1636; returned to England, 1636.

COMMISSARY JACOB HENDERSON (See *C.C.Del.*), sett. Annapolis, Md., 1713-1714; St. Paul's Parish, Md., 1714-1717; Leeland, Md., 1717-1751; Bsps. Comm. for Md., 1716-1723, 1729-1734; Ep.; d. Md., Aug. 27, 1751, a. 65.

FREDERICK LEWIS HENOP, b. Kaiserslautern, Palatinate, Oct. 7, 1740, son of a minister; matric. Heidelberg, Nov. 29, 1758; arriv. Am., 1765; sett. Northampton Co., Pa., as ffs., Dryland, Easton, Lehigh—St. Paul's Chh., Plainfield—St. Peter's Chh., 1765-1769; Durham (Bucks) Pa., 1765-1769; Greenwich (Berks) Pa., Dunkel Chh., 1765-1769; Greenwich (Warren) N. J., 1765-1769; Frederick,

Md., 1770-1784; Glades, Md., 1770-1784; Middletown (Frederick) Md., Zion or Kittatinny Chh., 1770-1784; and the ffg. in Va.; Lovettsville (Loudon), Stephentown (Frederick), Winchester (Frederick), Timberville, Roeder's Chh., Strasburg (Shenandoah) at Staufferstown, Woodstock (Shenandoah) at Millersville, 1770-1784; Germ. Ref.; d. Frederick, Md., late Sept. 1784.

HUGH HENRY, A.B., (See *C.C.Del.*), sett. Rehoboth, Md., 1751-1763; Salisbury, Md., 1751-1763; Princess Anne, Md., 1751-1763; Presb.; d. Rehoboth, Md., 1763.

JOHN HENRY, came from Ireland; Ord. Dublin, Ireland, 1710; arriv. Am., 1710; sett. Rehoboth (Somerset) Md., Pocomoke Chh., 1710-1717; Presb.; will dated Oct. 15, 1715; d. Rehoboth, Md., before Sept. 1717.

HENRY A SANCTO FRANCISCO, see Sancto Francisco.

JOHN HENRY HERTZER, b. Wuertemberg, Germany; came from Herrenhut; arriv. N. Y. C., Nov. 26, 1743; sett. Graceham, Md., 1745-1745; Warwick (Lanc.) Pa., Lititz, minister in rural districts; Lynn (Lehigh) Pa., 1747-1747; Moravian; d. Quittopehille (Lebanon) Pa., May, 1748.

JACOB HENDERSON HINDMAN, M.D., b. Queen Annes Co., Md.; Ord. 1769; K.B. Md., Mar. 24, 1770; sett. St. Andrew's Parish (St. Mary's) Md., as curate, 1772-1772; St. Peter's Parish (Talbot) Md., 1772-1780; Oxford, Md., 1772-1780; Great Choptank Parish (Dorchester) Md., 1773-1783; physician; Ep.; d. Great Choptank Parish, Md., after 1783.

JAMES HINDMAN, K.B. Md., Jan. 21, 1707/8; sett. St. Paul's Parish (Queen Annes) Md., 1710-1713; Ep.; d. St. Paul's Parish, Md., 1713; will made Aug. 10, 1713, proved Nov. 25, 1713.

ROBERT HODGSON, Quaker preacher, came on a missionary journey to Md., 1659; Friend.

ROBERT HODGSON, arriv. Md., 1713; S.J., R.C.; d. Bohemia Manor, Md., Dec. 18, 1726.

BASIL HOBART, arriv. Md., 1674; sett. Newport (Charles) Md., Hobart's Chapel, Franciscan, 1674-1698; R.C., d. Newport, Md., before July 10, 1698.

JOHN HOLBROKE, K.B., N. J., Dec. 13, 1723, as miss. S.P.G.; sett. Salem, N. J., 1723-1731; St. George's Parish (Harford) Md., 1725-1726; Hungar's Parish (Northampton) Va., 1729-1747; Ep.

CHRISTOPHER HOLDER, Quaker preacher from New England, came to Md. of a missionary journey, 1659; Friend.

ARTHUR HOLT, sett. All Faiths' Parish, Md., 1734-1734; Ep.

JOSEPH HOLT, A.B., b. Lancashire, Eng., 1668; adm. sizer, Jesus Coll., Cambridge, June 4, 1648, A.B., 1688/9; sett. Stratton-Major Parish (King and Queen) Va., 1696-1700; Petsworth (Gloucester) Va., 1697-1700; All Faiths' Parish (St. Mary's) Md., 1700-1703; St. Mary's City, Md., 1701-1705; William and Mary Parish, Md., 1701-1705; returned to Eng.; K.B. Barbadoes, Mar. 11, 1712/3; 1st miss. S.P.G. to the West Indies; Chaplain and physician at Barbadoes, 1712-1714; Ep.

HENRY HOOK (See *C.C.Del.*), sett. Chestertown, Md., 1737-1741; Presb.; d. Drawyer's Creek, Del., 1741.

JOSEPH HOUSTON, b. Ireland, 1693, educated in Scotland; Ord. Elk River (Cecil) Md., The Rock Chh., Oct. 15, 1724-1739; sett. Montgomery, N. Y., Good Will Chh., Jan. 1739/40-Oct. 29, 1740; Presb.; d. Wallkill, N. Y., Oct. 29, 1740, ae. 48.

JOHN HOWARD, lic. May 2, 1765; sett. Christ Church Parish (Queen Annes) Md., 1765-1775; Ep.

THOMAS HOWELL, prob. b. Llanboydy, Carmarthenshire, 1659; matric. Jesus Coll., Oxford, Mar. 9, 1676/7, perhaps rector of Heullan-Amgoed, Co. Carmarthen, Wales, 1681; sett. Dorchester Parish, Md., 1697-1708; Great Choptank Parish (Dorchester) Md., 1696-1727; Ep.

JOHN HUETT (See *C.C.Del.*), sett. Stepney Parish, Md., 1682-1695; Somerset Parish, Md., 1691-1695; Dorchester Parish, Md., 1691-1695; Ep.; d. Somerset Parish, Md., 1697/8.

PHILIP HUGHES, D.D., curate, Worcester Parish, Md., 1767-1768; induct. Chester Parish (Kent) Md., Aug. 7, 1769-Mar. 14, 1773; Ep.

JOHN HUMPHREY(S), A.B., b. Limerick, Ireland, 1683, son of Dr. Thomas Humphreys; sizar, Trinity Coll., Dublin, Nov. 13, 1699, a. 16; A.B., 1704; schoolmaster, N. Y., 1706-1710; Ord. by Bsp. of London, 1710; K.B. Pa., Nov. 3, 1710; sett. Oxford, Pa., Trinity Chh., 1711-1713, 1718-1719; S.P.G. missionary Chichester, Pa., 1713-1714, Marlborough, Pa., 1715-1726, Radnor, Pa., 1717-1718; sett. Chester, Pa., St. Peter's Chh., 1714-1726; Concord, Pa., St. John's Chh., 1714-1726; Marcus Hook, Pa., St. Martin's Chh., 1724-1729; St. George's Parish (Harford) Md., 1724-1725; sett. Annapolis, Md., St. Anne's Chh., Feb. 11, 1724/5-1739; Ep.; d. Annapolis, Md., July 8, 1739, ae. 53.

JAMES HUNT, A.M., b. Hanover Co., Va., 1731, son of James Hunt; A.B., Princeton, 1759, A.M.; Ord. New Brunswick Presbytery, N. J., 1761; sett. Rockville (Montgomery) Md., Bethany Chh., 1761-1793; Presb.; d. near Rockville, Md., June 2, 1793, ae. 62.

GEORGE HUNTER, sett. St. Thomas' Manor, Md., 1747; Charles County, Md., 1749; Port Tobacco, 1750; St. Inigoes, 1752; St. Thomas' Manor, 1755; ret. to England, 1756-1758; ret. from England, July 1, 1759; Superior, 1765; visited Canada, May 24, 1769; R.C.; d. St. Thomas' Manor, Md., Aug. 1, 1779.

HENRY HUNTER, sett. Pitt's Creek (Somerset) Md., ca. 1735; Presb.

SAMUEL HUNTER, K.B. Md., July 19, 1744; sett. Christ Chh. Parish (Queen Annes) Md., Kent Island, 1744-1746; All Saints' Parish

(Frederick) Md., Dec. 11, 1748-1759; Ep.; d. All Saints' Parish, Md., Oct. 1758.

WILLIAM HUNTER, b. Yorkshire, England, 1659; entered Soc. of Jesus, 1679; sett. Md., 1692; St. Mary's City, Md., 1692-1704; Port Tobacco (Charles) Md., St. Ignatius' Chapel, 1697-1723; Newport, Md., Jesuit Chapel, 1697-1723; Zekiah Swamp Creek (Charles) Md., Boarman Estate, 1697-1723; Superior, Md. R.C. Churches, 1696-1708; R.C.; d. Port Tobacco, Md., Aug. 15, 1723, a. 64.

ALEXANDER HUTCHINSON, from Glasgow Presbytery, Sept. 10, 1722, to Md.; Ord. Bohemia Manor (Cecil) Md., June 6, 1723-1766; Broad Creek, Md., 1723-1766; Presb.; d. Oct. 1766.

GEORGE IRWYN, K.B. Md., Aug. 24, 1716; sett. St. George's Parish (Harford) Md., 1716-1718; St. John's Parish (Baltimore) Md., Copley Parish, 1716-1718; Ep.

RICHARD JAMES, B.D., b. Somerset, Eng., ca. 1592; matric. Exeter Coll., Oxford, May 6, 1608, a. 16; scholar, Corpus Christi Coll., Oxford, 1608; A.B., Oct. 12, 1611, A.M., Jan. 24, 1614/5, Fellow, 1615, B.D., July 7, 1624; Librarian to Sir Robert Cotton, Eng., 1627; came to Va., 1628; sett. Kent Island, now Christ Church Parish (Queen Annes) Md., 1629-1638; returned to England, 1638; Ep.; bur. St. Margaret's, Westminster, Eng., Dec. 8, 1638.

AUGUSTINE JENKINS, arr. Md., May 24, 1774; R.C.; d. Newtown Manor, Md., Feb. 2, 1800.

HENRY JENNINGS (poss. b. Worcester, Eng., 1662, son of Robert Jennings, matric. Magdalen Hall, Oxford, Mar. 18, 1677/8, a. 16, A.B., 1681, clerk, Magdalen Coll., 1682-1685, A.M., 1684); sett. All Faiths' Parish (St. Mary's) Md., June 22, 1707-1709; William and Mary Parish, Md., 1706-1714; St. Mary's City, Md., 1706-1714; Ep.

JOSEPH JENNINGS, sett. All Saints' Parish (Frederick) Md., Nov. 23, 1742-1745; Ep.

THOMAS JOHNSON, sett. Prince George Parish (Montgomery) Md., as curate, 1758-1759; Ep.

HUGH JONES, A.M., b. Llanendwin, Merionethshire, 1671, son of Thomas Jones; matric. Gloucester Hall, Oxford, Nov. 15, 1694, a. 23; K.B. Md., Dec. 27, 1696; arriv. Md., 1696; sett. Christ Church Parish (Calvert) Md., at Port Republic, 1696-1702; prof. of Natural Philos. and Math., William and Mary Coll., Va., 1702-1722; sett. James City Parish (James City) Va., (1710?)-1720-1722; in England, 1722-1724; K.B. Va., Sept. 14, 1724; sett. St. Stephen's Parish (King and Queen) Va., 1724-Feb. 2, 1726; William and Mary Parish (Charles) Md., 1726-1730; All Faiths' Parish (St. Mary's) Md., 1730-1733; North Sassafras Parish (Cecil) Md., 1731-1760; Augustine Parish (Cecil) Md., 1744-1760; Ep.; d. North Sassafras Parish, Md., Sept. 8, 1760, ae. 91.

JOHN GEORGE JUNG (Young), educ. at Halle; arriv. Am., 1768; sett. Heidelberg (Lehigh) Pa., 1768-1768; North Whitehall (Lehigh) Pa., Schlosser's Chh., 1769-1772; South Whitehall, Pa., Jordon Chh., 1769-1772; Whitehall, Pa., Egypt Chh., 1771-1773; Chambersburg (Franklin) Pa., St. John's Chh., 1770-1783; Guilford (Franklin) Pa., Grindstone Chh., 1772-1783; Antietam, Md., 1773-1785; Hagerstown, Md., 1773-1793; Luth.

SAMUEL KEENE, D.D., b. Baltimore, Md., May 11, 1734; A.B., U. of Pa., 1759, A.M., 1765, Tutor, 1758-1759; D.D., Washington Coll., 1785; Ord. London, Sept. 29, 1760, lic. Sept. 30, 1760; sett. Annapolis, Md., St. Anne's Chh., Mar. 30, 1762-1767; St. Luke's Parish (Queen Annes) Md., Church Hill, July 27, 1767-1779, 1791-1803; Rector, Chester Parish (Kent) Md., 1779-1781; St. John's Parish (Caroline), 1781-1783; Dorchester Parish, Md., 1783-1791; St. Michael's Parish (Talbot) Md., 1805-1807; Ep.; d. St. Michael's Parish, Md., May 8, 1810, ae. 76.

ROBERT KEITH, K.B. Md., Apr. 25, 1701; sett. All Hallows' Parish (Worcester) Md., 1703-1707; Coventry Parish (Somerset) Md., 1703-1707; Ep.

JACOB KER, A.M., b. Freehold, N. J., son of Walter Ker; A.B., Princeton, 1758, A.M., Tutor, 1760-1762; Ord. 1763; sett. Princess Anne (Somerset) Md., Chh. at Manokin, Aug. 29, 1764-1795; Salisbury (Wicomico) Wicomico Chh., 1764-1795; Rehoboth (Somerset) Md., Pocomoke Chh., 1764-1779; Presb.; d. Manokin, Md., July 29, 1795.

JOHN KING (See *C.C.Del.*), sett. Eastern Shore, Md., Dec. 24, 1772; Frederick, Md., 1773; Meth.

JOHN KINGDOM, sett. Bohemia (Cecil) Md., St. Xavier's Chh., 1749-1760; R.C.; d. Port Tobacco, Md., 1761.

OWEN JOSEPH KINGSLEY, arriv. Md., 1739; returned to Europe; S.J., R.C.; d. Walten, Jan. 24, 1739/40, ae. 42.

JOHN CASPAR KIRCHNER, sett. Baltimore, Md., 1762-1773; Springfield (York) Pa., Frieden Saal or Shuster's Chh., 1763-1767; York, Pa., Christ Chh., 1763-1767; Luth.; d. Baltimore, Md., 1773.

RICHARD KIRKHAM, alias Latham, sett. Md., 1703-1709; S.J., R.C.

JOHN KNOLLES, arriv. Md., Aug. 8, 1637; sett. St. Mary's City, Md., 1637-1637; S.J., R.C.; d. Md., Oct. 1637.

JOHN VALENTINE KRAFT (See *C.C. Pa.*), sett. Monocacy, Md., 1750-1751; Luth.

OTTO CHRISTIAN KROGSTRUP, received a Univ. educ.; arriv. N. Y. C., Sept. 9, 1753; sett. Lancaster, Pa., 1754-1755, 1773-1776; Philadelphia, Pa., 1756-1762; Warwick (Lanc.) Pa., St. James's Chh. at Lititz, 1762-1763; Graceham, Md., 1764-1767; York, Pa., 1767-1773; Moravian; d. Bethlehem, Pa. 1785.

JOHN ANDREW KRUG, b. Saxony, Mar. 19, 1732; taught at the Orphan House at Halle, at Wasserleben and at Wernigerode; Ord. 1763; arriv. Philadelphia, Pa., Apr. 1, 1764; sett. Reading, Exeter, and Muhlenberg (all in Berks) Pa., 1764-1771, and Perry (Berks)

Pa., 1765-1771; Frederick, Md., Apr. 28, 1771-1796; Middletown, Md., 1771-1779; Luth.; d. Frederick, Md., Mar. 30, 1796.

ROBERT LAING (Lenig) (poss. son of Rev. Henry Laing (Layng) D.D., of Wells, Eng.; b. 1697; matric. Trinity Coll., Oxford, Mar. 28, 1713, ae. 13, A.B., Balliol, 1716, A.M., 1719); came from Great Britain to Md., 1722; member Presbytery of New Castle, Del.; sett. Snow Hill, Md., 1722; Brandywine and White Clay Creek, Del., Mar. 1722-Aug. 1722; sett. Bensalem (Bucks) Pa. and Warwick (Neshaminy Chh.), Dec. 22, 1723-1724; suspended for bathing on Sunday, Sept. 19, 1723, and again Sept. 24, 1726; the Presbytery advised him to quit the ministry.

CHARLES LAKE, sett. Annapolis, Md., Sept. 26, 1740-1743; St. James' Parish (Anne Arundel) Md., 1748-1753; Ep.

THOMAS LANDRUM (Lendrum), sett. St. George's Parish (Harford) Md., 1767-1770; Annapolis, Md., Jan. 16, 1775-1777; Ep.

JOHN LANG, K.B. Va., June 4, 1725; Ord. London, May, 1725; sett. St. Peter's Parish (New Kent) Va., 1725-1727; St. Luke's Parish (Queen Annes) Md., 1728-1734; St. James' Parish (Anne Arundel) Md., 1734-1749; Ep.; d. St. James' Parish, Md., 1748.

CHARLES LANGE, b. Innsbruck, Tyrol, 1731, of Catholic parentage; taught at Haldenstein; examined at Amsterdam, May 17, 1766; arriv. Am., 1766; sett. Frederick, Glades, Middletown and Taneytown, Md., 1766-1768; Lower Church, Peeked Mountain, Potomac Mountain, South Branch (or South Fork), Strasburg, Upper Church, Upper Tract and Woodstock, Va., 1766-May 1768; ejected from the Coetus, 1769; went to Va., 1769; German Reformed; d. ca. 1770.

FRANCIS LAUDER, prob. b. Md., lic. Nov. 24, 1761; Ord. 1761; sett. All Saints' Parish (Calvert) Md., 1761-1782; Christ Church Parish (Calvert) Md., 1761-1782; St. Andrew's Parish, Leonardstown, Md., 1764-1764; All Saints' Parish (Frederick) Md., 1782-1785; Ep.; d. All Saints' Parish (Frederick) Md., 1785.

ROBERT LAWSON, b. Scotland; member, Dumfries Presbytery, Dec. 1696; sett. Princess Anne, Manokin Chh., Md., 1713-1713; Salisbury, Wicomico Chh., 1713-1713; Presb.

JOHN LEACH, sett. St. Michael's Parish (Talbot) Md., 1692-1696; sett. St. Peter's Parish (Talbot) Md., 1692-1696; Ep.

DANIEL LEATHERMAN, Sen., sett. Hanover (York) Pa., Little Conewago Chh., 1738-1770; Monocacy (Frederick) Md., 1738-1770; Tunker or German Baptist.

THOMAS LECONBY, arriv., Md., 1734; S.J., R.C.; d. Port Tobacco, Md., Dec. 16, 1734.

BISHOP DANIEL LEHMAN, b. 1742, son of Bishop John Lehman; Ord. minister, 1775; Ord. Bishop, 1795; sett. Graceham, Md., Monocacy meeting, 1775-1804; Menn.; d. Chambersburg, Pa., 1804, ae. 62.

THE COLONIAL CLERGY OF MARYLAND 53

JAMES LE MOTTE, alias Lancaster, arr. Md., 1746; R.C.; d. Loretto, Italy, Dec. 3, 1756.

ANDREW LENDRUM, A.B., pens. Trinity Coll., Dublin, June 3, 1735; A.B., 1739; sett. Annapolis, Md., St. Anne's Chh., July, 1749-Sept. 26, 1749; St. George's Parish (Harford) Md., 1749-1767; Ep.

FREDERICK LEONARDS, arr. Md., 1760; R.C.; d. Port Tobacco, Md., Oct. 28, 1764.

JOHN LEWIS, sett. Bohemia, Md., 1750; sett. Whitemarsh (Baltimore) Md., St. Francis Borgia Chh., 1763-1773; Vicar-General, for Md., 1772; R.C.; d. Bohemia, Md., May 24, 1788.

JOHN LILLINGSTON, A.B., b. 1656, son of George Lillingston, of Kingsey, Bucks, Eng.; matric. Nov. 22, 1672, a. 16, A.B., 1676; Vicar of Ilmer, Bucks, Eng., 1677; K.B. Md., Oct. 29, 1689; sett. St. Peter's Parish (Talbot) Md., 1689-1691; St. Paul's Parish (Queen Annes) Md., 1691-1709; Ep.; d. St. Paul's Parish, Md., 1709.

JOHN JACOB LISCHY, b. Mulhouse, Alsace, France, May 28, 1719; arriv., Philadelphia, May 28, 1742; Ord. as a Moravian by Bishop Nitschmann, Jan. 1742/3; preacher to the following *Moravian* Churches in Pa.; Heidelberg, 1742-1743, Mt. Joy (Donegal Chh.), 1742-1745; Bethel (Lebanon Co.), Warwick (Lanc. Co.) St. James's Chh. at Lititz, 1743-1744; Swatara, South Lebanon Chh., 1743-1745; Lancaster, 1743-1746; Mill Creek (Leb.) Muehlbach Chh., 1743-1747; East Cocalico (Lanc.) Reamstown Chh., 1743-1748; York, 1744-1746; Hellam, 1746-1747; left the Moravian Chh., 1747; preached in the following *German Reformed* Chhs. in Pa.: East Coventry (Chester) Brownback's Chh., 1743-1744, Mill Creek (Leb.) Tulpehocken or Trinity Chh., 1743-1744; Brecknock, Muddy Creek Chh., 1743-1745; Bern (Berks), Jackson, Millbach Chh., Mt. Joy, Miller's Chh., 1743-1746; Ephrata, Bethany Chh., 1743-1747; West Cocalico, Swamp or Little Cocalico Chh., 1743-1748; Warwick, Kissel Hill Chh., 1743-1749; York, 1744-1761; Elizabeth, Whiteoaks Chh., 1745-1746; Codorus (York) St. Jacob's Chh., 1746-1748; Latimore (Adams) Long Green or Lower Bermudian, Mt. Olivet Chh., 1747-1761; Hellam, Kreutz Creek Chh., 1751-1757; Dover (York) Salem Chh., 1763-1781; West Manchester, St. Paul's or Wolf's Chh., 1763-1781; Lower Windsor, 1764-1765; North Codorus, St. Peter's or Lischy's Chh., 1765-1775; Paradise (York) Pa., Holy Schwamm Chh., 1775-1781; and Westminster, Md., St. Benjamin's or Krieger's Chh., 1763-1773; Swiss Refm., Moravian and Germ. Reform.; d. York Co., Pa., 1781.

ARNOLD LIVERS, sett. St. Thomas' Manor, Md., 1733-1737; Newtown, 1742; S.J., R.C.; d. St. Inigoes, Md., Aug. 16, 1777.

HENRY LOVEALL, b. Cambridge, England, 1694 (his real name was Desolate Baker), sett. Newport, R. I., 1729-1730; Ord. Piscataway, N. J., Chh. at Stilton, Raritan, 1730-1742; Chestnut

Ridge, Md., Sater's Chh., Fall's Road, 1742-1772; Opequon (Berkeley) W. Va., Mill Creek Chh., 1746-1751; Gen. Bapt.; living at Chestnut Ridge, Md., 1772, ae. 78 yrs.

DAVID LOW, K.B. Md., Apr. 12, 1764; sett. All Hallows' Parish (Anne Arundel) Md., 1764-1775; Ep.

JOHN LUCAS, came from England, 1770; R.C.; d. Sept. 11, 1794.

NEVIL MACCALLUM, K.B. Va., Sept. 11, 1735; sett. Dorchester Parish (Dorchester) Md., 1741-1770; Ep.

ALEXANDER McDOWALL (See *C.C.Del.*), Elk River, Md., Rock Chh. at Lewisville, 1744-1760; Bethel (Harford) Md., Chh. at Upper Node Forest, 1774; Presb.; d. Newark, Del., Jan. 12, 1782, unm.

DANIEL McGILL, came from England, 1713; sett. Bladensburg, Md., 1713-1719; Upper Marlborough (Prince George) Md., on Patuxent River, 1713-1719; supplied at various places in Md., Del. and Va., 1719-1724; Presb.; d. London Tract (New Castle) Del., Feb. 10, 1724.

JAMES MACGILL, b. Scotland, lic. Mar. 28, 1727, K.B. Md., Apr. 11, 1728; sett. Somerset Parish (Somerset) Md., Princess Anne and Monie, 1727-1730; Queen Caroline Parish (Howard) Md., St. John's Chh., Guilford, 1730-1778; Vicount Oxford, Lord MACGILL of Cowsland; Ep.; d. Queen Caroline Parish, Md., Dec. 26, 1779.

DANIEL McKENNON, lic. for Md., Dec. 22, 1768; K.B. Md. Jan. 19, 1769; sett. All Saints' Parish (Frederick) Md., 1769-Jan. 1774; Westminster Parish (Anne Arundel) Md., Jan. 1774-1776; Ep.; returned to England during the Revolution and was lost at sea.

ROBERT McMORIDE, Ord. Cumberland (Adams) Pa., Upper Marsh Creek Chh., Gettysburg, 1754-Jan. 1761; Hopewell (York) Pa., Shrewsbury Chh., Round Hill, 1754-Jan. 1761; East Hanover (Dauphin) Pa., 1762-1766; Baltimore, Md., 1774-1774; miss. to Va. and Carolina, 1772-1784; Chaplain, Rev. War; member, Ord. of the Cincinnati; Presb.; d. May 22, 1796.

GEORGE MACNISH, educ. in Scotland; sett. Va., 1705; lic. June 1706; sett. Princess Anne (Somerset) Md., Manokin Chh., 1710-1711; Salisbury (Wicomico) Md., Wicomico Chh., 1710-1711; Jamaica, L. I., N. Y., Jan. 25, 1712-1723; Presb.; d. Newtown, L. I., N. Y., Mar. 10, 1722/3.

WILLIAM MACONCHIE (Machonchie), b. Scotland; K.B. Md., Oct. 10, 1710; sett. Durham Parish (Charles) Md., Chh. at Nanjemoy, 1711-1742; Port Tobacco Parish (Charles), Md., 1711-1742; Ep.; d. Port Tobacco Parish, Md., 1742.

JOHN McPHERSON, D.D., b. Scotland, ca. 1725; Ord. 1751; lic. Apr. 17, 1751; K.B. Md., Apr. 18, 1751; sett. Annapolis, Md., St. Anne's Chh., July 20, 1755-1756; William and Mary Parish (Charles) Md., 1756-1785; Ep.; d. William and Mary Parish, Md., 1785, ae. ca. 60.

WALTER MAGOWAN, b. Ireland, ca. 1736; Ord. 1768; lic. for Va., June 24, 1768; K.B. Va., June 30, 1768; sett. St. James' Parish (Anne Arundel) Md., Herring Creek, 1769-1786; Ep.; d. St. James' Parish, Md., 1786, ae. ca. 50.

FRANCIS MAKEMIE, b. near Ramelton, Donegal, Ireland, 1658; matric. U. of Glasgow, Feb. 1675/6; Ord. Presbytery of Lagan, Ireland, 1682; sett. Rehoboth (Somerset) Md., Pocomoke Chh., 1683-1708; Snow Hill (Worcester) Md., 1683-1688 (and perhaps 1683-1708); Accomac (Accomac) Va., 1688-1708; first Presb. minister in Am.; moderator of the first Presbytery in Am., Dec. 1706; d. Matchatank (Accomac) Va., summer 1708, ae. 50 (will made Apr. 27, 1708; proved Aug. 4, 1708).

ALEXANDER MALCOLM, sett. Annapolis, Md., Dec. 5, 1749-1754; St. Paul's Parish (Queen Annes) Md., 1754-1763; Chaplain, Md. Assembly; Ep.; d. St. Paul's Parish, Md., June 15, 1763.

MATTHIAS MANNERS, alias Sittensperger, sett. Conewago, Pa., 1753-1771; Bohemia Manor, Md., 1771; R.C.; d. Bohemia Manor, June 15, 1775.

PETER MANNERS, alias Pelcon, sett. Md., 1664-1669; S.J., R.C.; d. Md., Apr. 24, 1669.

THOMAS MANSELL, b. Oxfordshire, 1669; adm. S.J., June, 1686; Ord. ca. 1700; arriv. Md., 1700; sett. Bohemia (Cecil) Md., St. Xavier's mission, 1706-1724, near the junction of Great and Little Bohemia Rivers at Bohemia Manor; Superior, Jesuit Order in Md., 1714-1724; d. Bohemia Manor, Md., Mar. 18, 1724, a. 55.

RICHARD MARSDEN, A.M. (or Marston), sett. St. Michael's Parish (Talbot) Md., 1696-1707; Rector, Charleston, S. C., St. Philip's Chh., 1707-1708; Christ Chh. Parish (Berkeley) S. C., Aug. 9, 1708-1709; returned to Eng., 1709; came to Va. without a Bishop's certificate; sett. Lynnhaven (Princess Anne) Va., Jan. 7, 1729-Nov. 14, 1729; left Lynnhaven £400 in debt; sett. St. James' Parish (New Hanover) N. C., 1729-1742; S.P.G. missionary in Cape Fear region, N. C., 1738; Ep.; d. near Wilmington, N. C., 1742.

GEORGE ADAM MARTIN, b. Landstuhl, Germany, 1715; Ord. 1739; sett. Reading (Adams) Pa., Great Conewago Chh., 1741-1770; Latimore (Adams) Pa., Bermudian Chh., 1762-1770; Antietam, Md., 1763-1770; Brothertown (Somerset) Pa., Stony Creek Chh., 1770-1776; Dunkard, Tunker or German Bapt.; d. Ephrata, Pa., Apr. 29, 1794.

NICHOLAS MARTIN, sett. Conococheague, Md., ca. 1770; Hanover (York) Pa., Little Conewago Chh., ca. 1770; Reading (Adams) Pa., Great Conewago Chh., ca. 1770; Dunkard, Tunker or German Bapt.

THOMAS MARTIN, Ord. Oct. 12, 1697; sett. Upper Providence (Montgomery) Pa., 1697-1700; Newton (Delaware) Pa., 1697-1701; Nottingham, Md., 1700; Keithian Bapt. or Seventh Day Bapt.

LEIGH MASSEY, A.B., b. 1700, son of James Massey of Oxmantown near Dublin, Ireland; matric. Brasenose Coll., Oxford, May 30, 1718, ae. 18; A.B., Jan. 31, 1721/2; K.B. Md., Nov. 1, 1722; sett. William and Mary Parish (St. Mary's) Md., 1723-1733; St. Mary's City, Md., 1723-1733; Ep.; d. St. Mary's City, Md., Jan. 10, 1732/3.

MASSEUS MASSEY A SANTA BARBARA, arriv. Md., 1673; sett. Newport (Charles) Md., Franciscan Chapel, 1680-1684; Superior of the Franciscan missions, 1680-1684; Guardian at Gronow, Douay; Vicar, Minister and Commissary General of the Province of Md.; R.C.

JOSEPH MATHER, A.M., b. Chester, Pa., son of John Mather; U. Pa., 1757, but did not grad., A.M., 1762; Ord. Eng., 1760; lic. Dec. 29, 1760; K.B. Md., Jan. 8, 1761; sett. Augustine Parish (Cecil) Md., 1761-1774; Ep.

IGNATIUS MATTHEWS, arr. Md., 1765, sett. Deer Creek (Harford) Md., St. Joseph's Chapel, 1770-1779; S.J., R.C.; d. Newtown, Md., May 11, 1790.

JOHN MATTHEWS, arriv. Md., 1694; S.J., R.C.; d. Newtown, Md., Dec. 8, 1694.

DANIEL MAYNADIER, A.B., b. Occitania, 1673, son of Daniel Maynadier, gent.; sizar, Trinity Coll., Dublin, July 14, 1694, a. 21; A.B., 1699; K.B. Narragansett, R. I., Nov. 13, 1711; sett. Westminster Parish (Anne Arundel) Md., 1712-1714; St. Peter's Parish (Talbot) Md., May 1714-1745; (also Oxford (Talbot) Md., 1716-1745, unless the Samuel Maynadier who follows actually existed); Ep.; of Huguenot descent.

DANIEL MAYNADIER, JR., M.D., son of the Rev. Daniel Maynadier; Ord. 1760; lic. Dec. 29, 1760; K.B. Md., Jan. 15, 1761; sett. Great Choptank Parish (Dorchester) Md., at Cambridge, 1765-1772; physician; Ep.; d. Great Choptank Parish, Md., 1772.

SAMUEL MAYNADIER (perhaps brother of Daniel, Sen., or more probably identical with him), came to Md. before 1713; sett. Oxford, Md., 1716-1745; Ep.; d. Oxford, Md., late in 1745.

JOSEPH MESSENGER, b. Eng., ca. 1747; Ord. 1772; lic. for Stafford Co., Va., May 7, 1772; K.B. Va., May 19, 1772; sett. Overwharton Parish, Va., 1772-1774; St. Andrew's Parish (St. Mary's City) Md., 1775-1780; William and Mary Parish (St. Mary's) Md., 1780-1786; St. John's Parish (Prince George) Md., 1786-1806; Ep.; d. St. John's Parish, Md., 1810, a. ca. 63.

RICHARD MOLYNEUX, came to Md., 1733; sett. St. Thomas' Manor, 1737-1749; Superior, 1736, *et seq.*; ret. to England, 1749; S.J., R.C.; d. England, May 17, 1766.

ROBERT MOLYNEUX, arr. Md., 1767; R.C.; at Philadelphia, 1774.

JOHN MONTGOMERY, A.M., A.B., U. of Pa., 1766, A.M.; Tutor, 1766-1769; K.B. Md., Aug. 16, 1770; sett. Worcester Parish

(Worcester) Md., 1770-1772; Annapolis, Md., St. Anne's Chh., Jan. 21, 1772-1775; inducted, Shrewsbury Parish (Kent) Md., Feb. 7, 1775-1777; Wye Mills (Talbot) Md., 1775-1777; St. Mary's Chh., Burlington, N. J., 1777; returned to England; Ep.; d. Hereford, England, 1802.

MR. MOORE (first name unknown), sett. Port Tobacco Parish (Charles) Md., 1691-1692; Durham Parish, Md., 1691-1692; William and Mary Parish (Charles) Md., at Nanjemoy, 1692-1692; Ep.; d. 1692.

MOUSIUR MORIEN (Monsieur?), sett. St. Paul's Parish (Prince George) Md., 1696-(1696?); Ep.

PETER MORRIS, arr. Md., 1767; R.C.; d. Newtown, Md., Nov. 19, 1782.

JOSEPH MOSLEY, sett. Newton (St. Mary's) Md., 1759-1767, St. Xavier's Chh.; Newport (Charles) Md., Jesuit Chapel, 1760-1787; Zekiah Swamp Creek (Charles) Md., Boarman Estate, 1759-1763; Bohemia Manor (Cecil) Md., St. Xavier's Chh., 1760-1787; St. Joseph's Parish (Talbot) Md., 1764-1787; S.J., R.C.; d. 1787.

WILLIAM MULLETT, D.D., arriv. Md., 1683; sett. Christ Church Parish (Calvert) Md., at Port Republic, 1684-(1693?); Ep.

GEORGE MURDOCK (sometimes given as William Murdock); Ord. London by Bishop of London, Feb. 29, 1724; sett. Prince George Parish (Montgomery) Md., at that time including all of western Md., Dec. 29, 1726-1761; Rock Creek Parish, Md. (now Washington, D. C.), 1726-1761; Ep.; d. Prince George Parish, Md., Feb. 1761.

MICHAEL MURPHY, arr. Md., 1754; sett. Newtown Manor, 1755-1759; R.C.; d. Newtown, Md., 1759.

BENEDICT NEALE, grandson of Capt. James Neale; sett. Deer Creek (Harford) Md., St. Joseph's Chapel, 1747-1770; took a land patent of 120 acres in Washington, Pa., 1747; S.J., R.C.; d. Newtown, Md., Mar. 20, 1787.

HUGH NEILL, A.M. (See *C.C.Del.*), sett. St. Paul's Parish (Queen Annes) Md., 1765-1781; Presb.-Ep.; d. Oxford, Pa., 1781.

GEORGE NEISSER, b. Sehlen, Moravia, Apr. 11, 1715; arriv. Savannah, Ga., Feb. 16, 1735/6; Philadelphia, Feb. 1737; Bethlehem, Pa., June 25, 1742, where he was the first schoolmaster, diarist, clerk, postmaster, lawyer and musician; sett. N. Y., N. Y., 1742-1748, 1765-1777; Graceham, Md., 1748-1748; Ord. 1748; Lancaster, Pa., 1751-1753; York, Pa., 1756-1757; Warwick, Pa., St. James' Chh. at Lititz, 1757-1759; Philadelphia, Pa., 1762-1774; Moravian; d. Philadelphia, 1784.

JOSEPH NEISSER, Ord. in Europe; arriv. Bethlehem, Nov. 28, 1765; sett. Graceham, Md., 1771-1775; Hope (Warren) N. J., 1775-1776; Moravian.

(DOMINE) NEWBURG, sett. Manchester (Carroll) Md., Zion Chh., 1760-1783; Luth.

HENRY NICOLS, A.M. (Nichols or Nicholls), b. Apr. 1, 1678, son of Jonathan Nichols of Cowbridge, Glamorgan; matric. Jesus Coll., Oxford, Mar. 11, 1696/7, a. 16; A.B., 1701, A.M., Mar. 28, 1715; Fellow; K.B. May 5, 1703; missionary V.S.P.G.; Concord, Pa., 1703-1708; Marcus Hook, Pa., 1703-1708; Chester, Pa., 1704-1708; Newton, Pa., Radnor, 1704-1708; St. Michael's Parish (Talbot) Md., 1708-1749; Ep.; d. St. Michaels, Md., Feb. 12, 1749.

GEORGE NIEKE, came from Herrenhut, Moravia; arriv. N. Y. C., Nov. 26, 1743; Ord. Oley, Pa., as deacon, Mar. 1, 1744; sett. Graceham, Md., 1746-1748; Monocacy, Md., 1746-1748; minister in rural districts; Moravian.

BENJAMIN NOBBS, K.B. Md., Jan. 11, 1697/8; sett. William and Mary Parish (St. Mary's) Md., 1698-1700; All Faiths' Parish, Md., 1698-1707; St. Mary's City, Md., 1698-1700; Ep.

ABEL NOBLE, b. Bristol, R. I., son of William and Frances Noble from Bristol, England; brought up as a Quaker; came to Pa. ca. 1684, as a Friend; became a 7th Day or Keithian Baptist, 1691; sett. Newtown, Pa., 1697-1701; Nottingham, Pa., 1697-1700; only 7th Day Baptist minister in Pa. ca. 1700; he served for many years, date of death is given as 1775, obviously incorrect.

LAWRENCE (Lorenz or Laurentius) THORSTANSEA NYBERG, educ. at Upsala, Sweden; Ord. Sweden, 1743; excluded from the Swedish Lutheran ministry; preached in Lutheran Chhs. as ffs.: Hanover (York) Pa., St. Michael's Chh., 1743-1744; Warwick, Pa., St. James' Chh., 1744-1746; Lancaster, Pa., Trinity Luth. Chh., 1744-1746; York, Pa., Christ Chh., 1744-1748; Monocacy, Md., 1745-1746; also by tradition, Conewago (Adams) Pa., 1744-1748; had been preaching for some time in Moravian Chhs., and on Aug. 13, 1748, he became a Moravian, and was Ord. London, 1754; preached in Moravian Chhs. as ffs.: Warwick, Pa., 1744-1745; Graceham, Md., 1745-1745; York, Pa., 1744-1748; Swatara, Pa., South Lebanon Chh., 1745-1750; Lancaster, Pa., 1746-1748; Old Man's Creek (Gloucester) N. J., at Pilesgrove, Woolwich, 1747-1749; returned to England, 1750; Sw. Luth.; Luth.; Moravian.

HENRY OGLE (K.B. W. Indies, Dec. 7, 1704; Ord. for Va., Apr. 5, 1705?), sett. Durham Parish (Charles) Md., 1743-1750; Port Tobacco Parish, Md., 1743-1750; returned to England, 1750; Ep.

JOHN ORME, came from Devonshire, Eng., to Md., Sept. 26, 1720; sett. Upper Marlborough, on Patuxent River, Md., 1720-1758; Old Side Presb.; d. Upper Marlborough, Md., 1758.

WILLIAM ORR, A.M., b. Ireland; memb. New Castle Presbytery, Nov. 15, 1730; Ord. Nottingham, Pa. (Presb.), before 1732; sett. Lower West Nottingham, Md., Lower Octorara Chh., 1732-1735; turned Episcopalian; Ord. by Bshp. of London, Sept. 29, 1736; K.B. S. C., Oct. 7, 1736; arriv. S. C., 1737; sett. Charleston, S. C., St. Philip's Chh., Jan. 20, 1736/7-1741; St. Paul's Parish (Colleton) S. C., 1741-1744; St. Helena's Parish (Beaufort) S. C., 1746-1747; St. John's

Parish (Colleton) S. C., May, 1750-1755; preacher, 10th visitation, 1740; Presb.-Ep.; d. St. Paul's Parish, Colleton, S. C., 1755.

BISHOP PHILIP WILHELM OTTERBEIN, b. Dillenburg, Nassau, Germany, June 3, 1726, son of Rev. John Daniel and Wilhelmina Henrietta (Hoerlen) Otterbein; Herborn Seminary, 1742; Ord. (Germ. Ref.) Ockersdorf, Germany, June 13, 1749, where he was vicar; arr. N. Y. C., July 28, 1752; sett. Lancaster, Pa., Aug. 1752-1758; Pequea, Pa., 1752-1758; Mill Creek (Lebanon) Pa., Old Tulpehocken Chh., 1758-1760; Tulpehocken (Berks) Pa., Host Chh., 1758-1760; Conococheague, Md., St. Paul's Chh., 1760-1765; Frederick, Md., 1760-1765; Middletown, Md., 1760-1765; Hellam, Pa., Kreutz's Chh., 1765-1770; Conewago (York) Pa., Zion's or Quickel's Chh., 1765-1774; Lower Windsor (York) Pa., 1765-1774; Paradise (York) Pa., 1765-1774; Union (Adams) Pa., 1765-1774; York, Pa., Nov. 1765-1774; Hopewell (York) Pa., 1767-1774; Antietam, Md., 1774-1783; Baltimore, Md., 2nd Chh., 1774-1813; founder of the United Brethren in Christ; German Reformed Bishop; d. Baltimore, Md., Oct. 17, 1813, a. 87.

RICHARD OWEN, b. U. S. A., lic. ca. 1772; sett. Baltimore, Md., 1772; Meth.

ROBERT OWEN (prob. b. 1674, son of Robert Owen, of Glamorgan; matric. Jesus Coll., Oxford, Mar. 13, 1692/3, a. 18; K.B. Md., Aug. 31, 1699; sett. Piscataway Parish (Prince George) Md., 1699-1700; St. Paul's Parish (Prince George) Md., 1700-1710; "was called to England upon hopes of an estate, but being disappointed, he is desirous to return to Maryland, Sept. 13, 1705"; Ep.; living in Md., 1714.

JOHN PATTERSON, K.B. Md., June 14, 1768; sett. Chester Parish (Kent) Md., as curate, 1769-1773; Rector, 1773-1775; Ep.

JOHN PAUL, b. Ireland, 1706; lic. Dec. 10, 1735; instal. Lower West Nottingham, Md., Lower Octoraro Chh., Oct. 1736-1739; Presb.; d. Lower West Nottingham, Pa., 1739, ae. 33.

HENRY PAULTON, arriv. Md., 1712; S.J., R.C.; d. Newtown Manor, Md., Sept. 17, 1712.

THOMAS PAYTON, sett. Md., 1658-1659; S.J., R.C.; d. N. Y. C., Jan. 12, 1660.

DUELL PEAD, A.B., bapt. Westminster Abbey, London, Eng., Apr. 18, 1663; adm. pens. Trinity Coll., Cambridge, 1664, A.B.; Ord. by Bsp. of London, May 17, 1668; came from Eng. to Va., 1683; sett. All Hallows' Parish (Anne Arundel) Md., 1683-1690; Christ Chh. Parish (Middlesex) Va., 1683-1690; St. Mary's City, Md., 1683-1685; William and Mary Parish (St. Mary's) Md., 1683-1685; returned to Eng.; Chaplain to Duke of Newcastle; sett. St. James', Clerkenwell, 1691-1727; sett. as Rector of Newland, St. Lawrence, Essex, Eng., 1707-1710; author; Ep.; d. Jan. 12, 1726/7, buried at Clerkenwell.

JAMES PELLENTZ, sett. Lancaster, Pa., 1758-1768; sett. Frederick, Md., 1768-1770; R.C.

FRANCIS PENNINGTON, arriv. Md., 1675; sett. Newtown (St. Mary's) Md., St. Francis Xavier Chh., 1675-1699; Superior; S.J., R.C.; d. Newtown, Md., Feb. 22, 1699.

JOHN PENNINGTON, arriv. Md., 1684; S.J., R.C.; d. Newtown, Md., Oct. 18, 1685.

THOMAS PERCY, in Md., 1682; S.J., R.C.; returned to England, 1683.

THOMAS PHILLIPS, sett. Basseterre, St. Christopher, West Indies, and Newfoundland; K.B. Va., Aug. 9, 1715; sett. in a "Parish of Potomac River," 1716 (which must have been Overwharton Parish (Stafford) Va.); sett. Christ Church Parish (Queen Annes) Md., 1719-1731; Ep.

VINCENT PHILLIPS, served in Md., 1733-1746; S.J., R.C.; d. St. Mary's Co., Md., 1748.

CHRISTOPHER PLATTS, sett. King and Queen Parish (St. Mary's) Md., 1696-1700; Ep.

GEORGE POLE, in Md., 1666-1669; S.J., R.C.; d. Md., Oct. 31, 1669.

JOHN PORTER, K.B. Md., June 14, 1768; sett. St. George's Parish (Harford) Md., 1769-1770; Ep.

FERDINAND POULTER (or Poulton, alias John Brock or Morgan), b. Buckinghamshire, Eng., ca. 1600; adm. S.J., 1622; sett. St. Mary's City, Md., 1638-1640; St. Inigoes (St. Mary's) Md., Chh. of the Assumption, 1638-1640; Superior of missions; S.J., R.C.; d. St. Mary's City, Md., 1641.

THOMAS POULTER (or Poulton), arriv., Md., 1738; sett. Bohemia Manor, Md., 1742-1749; R.C.; d. Newtown Manor, Md., Jan. 23, 1749/50.

JAMES QUIN, sett. Anne Arundel Co., 1733-1738; S.J., R.C.; d. Choptank River, Md., Nov. 27, 1745.

GILES RAINSFORD, A.M., b. Dublin, Ireland, 1679, son of Mark Rainsford; pens. Trinity Coll., Dublin, Apr. 2, 1695, a. 16; A.B., 1699, A.M., 1705; Fellow Commoner, St. John's Coll., Cambridge, Mar. 23, 1699/1700; Ord. by Bsp. of London, 1702; K.B. Jamaica, June 15, 1702; miss. S.P.G. at Edenton (Chowan) N. C., St. Paul's Chh., 1712-1714; sett. East or Lower Parish (Nansemond) Va., 1714-1716; returned to Eng., 1716; K.B. Md., Sept. 3, 1716; came back to Va.; sett. St. Anne's Parish (Essex) Va., 1717-1718; also Culpeper Co., 1718-1720; St. Paul's Parish (Prince George), Md., 1720-1724; Ep.

JOHN RANKIN (See *C.C.Del.*), sett. Buckingham, Md., Berlin, Eastern Shore, 1775-1798; Presb.; d. Buckingham, Md., Mar. 2, 1798, a. 48.

THOMAS READ, b. Va. ca. 1748; Ord. 1773; K.B. Md., Sept. 25, 1773; sett. Prince George Parish (Montgomery) Md., 1773-1777,

1780-1816; Annapolis, Md., St. Anne's Chh., 1777-1780; Ep.; d. Prince George Parish, Md., 1838, a. 90.

ROBERT READE, lic. for Va., Apr. 10, 1758; called to Petsworth Parish (Gloucester) Va., 1762, but did not accept; sett. Coventry Parish (Somerset) Md., curate, 1762-1770; St. Paul's Parish (Kent) Md., 1775-1778; Kingston Parish (Mathews) Va., 1778 et seq.; Ep.

PHILIP READING (See *C.C.Del.*), sett. Augustine Parish (Cecil) Md., 1774-1776; Ep.; d. Appoquinimink, Del., Oct. 29, 1778.

ROBERT RENNY (Ranney), K.B. Va., July 11, 1764; lic. July 1, 1764 for Va.; curate, St. Andrew's Parish (St. Mary's) Md., 1764-1767; Ep.

MATTHEW REUTZ (See *C.C.Del.*), sett. Graceham, Md., 1751-1751; Moravian; d. Old Man's Creek, N. J., Oct. 7, 1753.

JOSEPH RHEA, b. Ireland, ca. 1715; sett. Cumberland (Adams) Pa., Upper Marsh Creek Chh., at Gettysburg, 1770-1771; Taneytown, Md., Piney Creek Chh., 1771-Apr. 11, 1776; Presb.; d. Va., Sept. 20, 1777, a. ca. 62.

WILLIAM RICHARDSON, was recognized as a Quaker preacher at West River, Md., 1679; Friend.

JOHN CHRISTIAN RICHTER, arriv. N. Y. C., May 12, 1749; sett. Graceham, Md., 1755-1757; Moravian.

ROGER RIGBY, arriv. Md., 1641; sett. Patuxent, Md., Indian mission, 1641-1646; R. C.; d. Va., 1646.

JAMES ROBERTSON, K.B., Va., Jan. 15, 1717/8; attended Convocation at Williamsburg, Va., 1719; sett. Westover Parish (Charles City) Va., 1718-1720; Coventry Parish (Somerset) Md., Ep.

WILLIAM ROBERTSON, Quaker preacher; came on a missionary journey to Md., 1659; Friend.

LEWIS BENJAMIN ROELS, arr. in Md., June 24, 1761; R.C.; d. St. Thomas' Manor, Md., Feb. 27, 1794.

GEORGE ROFE, a Recognized Quaker preacher in Md., 1661; ministered there, 1661, and "found many settled meetings in Maryland"; Friend.

FRANCIS ROGERS, in Md., 1654; returned to Europe soon; S.J., R.C.

JOHN ROGERS, alias Bamfield, sett. Md., 1636-1638; S.J., R.C.

ISAAC ROLLINS, Eastern Shore, Md., Dec. 24, 1772; Chester Circuit, Pa., 1773; Meth.; d. Yellow Springs, Chester Co., Pa., 1783.

SVEN ROSEEN, b. Torpa, West Gothland, Sweden, 1708; educ. at Upsala and Jena Univ., theol. stud. at Upsala and Lindheim, 1744, a. 36; arriv. Bethlehem, Pa., Jan. 12, 1747/8; Ord. deacon, 1748; sett. Graceham, Md., 1749-1750; Bethlehem, Pa., Brodhead settlement at Dansbury, 1749-1750; Lynn (Lehigh) Pa., Allemaengel Chh., 1748-1750; Paulin's Kill and Wallpack, N. J., 1749-1750; and as an itinerant preacher at Ammasland, Darby Creek, Pa., Bridgeton, Cohansey

Chh., N. J., Calkoen's Hook, Pa., Pennsneck, Quihawken, N. J., Swedesboro, Raccoon Chh. and Swedish Settlements, N. J., 1748-1750; Cape May, N. J., 1748-1749; Great Egg Harbor, Little Egg Harbor and Mauris River, N. J., 1749-1750; Moravian; d. Macungie, Pa., Dec. 15, 1750.

GEORGE ROSS, A.M. (See *C.C.Del.*), sett. North Elk Parish (Cecil) Md., 1731-1735; Ep.; d. New Castle, Del., 1753, ae. 72.

JOHN ROSSE, A.M., son of George Ross (A.M., Corpus Christ Coll., Cambridge, 1720, Merton Coll., Oxford, 1722); lic. Sept. 22, 1754; K.B. Md., Oct. 10, 1754; sett. All Hallows' Parish (Worcester) Md., 1754-1775; Ep.

HENRY A SANCTO FRANCISCO, arriv. Md., 1676; sett. Newport (Charles) Md., 1676-1676; Franciscan; R.C.

JOHN HELFRICH SCHAUM, b. Giessen, Hesse-Darmstadt, Germany, son of John Philip H. Schaum; educ. U. of Halle; arriv. Philadelphia, Pa., Jan. 26, 1744/5; arriv. York, Pa., May 17, 1748; Ord. Lancaster, Pa., June 4, 1749; sett. Cohansey and Somerset, N. J., 1746-1747; Raritan, N. J., 1747-1748; York, Pa., Christ Chh., May 17, 1748-Apr. 1755; Latimore (Adams) Pa., Lower Bermudian Chh., 1748-1755; Hanover (York) Pa., St. Michael's Chh., 1748-1752; Frederick, Md., 1752-1755; Bedminster (Bucks) Pa., Keller's Chh., Apr. 1755-1759; Upper Dublin (Montg.) Pa., Puff's Chh., 1758-1762; New Hanover (Montg.) Pa., Falkner's Swamp Chh., 1759-1762; Douglass (Berks) Pa., Oley Hill Chh., 1759-1762; Oley (Berks) Pa., Christ or Hill Chh., 1759-1778; Pike, Pa., St. John's or Hill Chh., 1759-1778; Upper Providence (Montgomery) Pa., Augustus Chh. at Trappe, 1759-1778; Amity, Pa., St. Paul's Chh., 1761-1767; Richmond, Pa., Zion or Moselem Chh., 1761-1778; North Whitehall (Lehigh) Pa., Schlosser's Chh., 1762-1769; Rockland (Berks) Pa., Bieber Creek Chh., 1759-1778; Luth., d. Rockland, Pa., Jan. 26, 1788.

MICHAEL SCHLATTER, b. St. Gall, Switzerland, July 14, 1716, son of Paulus and Magdalena (Zollikofer) Schlatter; educ. gymnasium, St. Gall; matric. U. Leyden, Dec. 27, 1736, and Helmstedt, Brunswick, Germany; Ord. St. Gall, Apr. 10, 1739; Rector, Wigoldingen, Switzerland, 1744-1745; Linzebuehl near St. Gall, Aug. 19, 1745-Jan. 1746; agent to the German Chhs. in Pa., 1746; arriv. Boston, Mass., Aug. 1, 1746; arriv. Philadelphia, Sept. 6, 1746; sett. Lancaster, Pa., 1746-1746; Northampton (Bucks) Pa., Dutch Reformed Chh., 1746-1750, Neshaminy Chh. (G.R.), 1748-1750; Southampton (Bucks) Pa., Dutch Ref. Chh., Churchville, 1746-1752; North and Southampton Chhs., (G.R.), 1748-1750; Upper Providence, Pa., St. Luke's Chh. at Trappe, 1746-1746; Penn, Pa., Unionville Chh., 1747-1747; Union (Adams) Pa., 1747-1747; Frederick, Md., 1747-1748; Lebanon (Hunterdon) N. J., Rockaway Chh. at Clinton, 1747-1750; Philadelphia, Pa., and Germantown, Pa., 1747-1751; Whitpain, Boehm's Chh., 1749-1756; Reading, Pa., 1754-1754; Whitemarsh, Pa., St. Peter's Chh., Barren Hill, 1759-1777; went to Holland, Feb. 5, 1751-May 12, 1752; to Europe, Nov. 28, 1753-Sept.

28, 1754; Supt. of Charity Schools in the Colonies, 1754-1757; Chaplain, appointed Mar. 25, 1757, at Louisbourg and Fort Duquene, 1757-1759; Chaplain, 2nd Pa. Battalion, 1764; Germ. Reformed; d. Philadelphia, Oct. 31, 1790.

JOHANNES SCHWEISHAUPT (Schweisshaupt or Schweitzhaupt), arriv. N. Y. C., May 12, 1749; sett. Salisbury (Lehigh) Pa., Emaus Chh., 1758-1760; Mt. Joy, Donegal Chh., 1763-1774; Graceham, Md., 1775-1784; Moravian; his wife, Magdalena, was also ordained.

JOHN WILLIAM SAMUEL SCHWERDTFEGER, b. near Neustadt on the Aisel, Mittelfranken, Bavaria, 1722, an orphan, stud. theol. and law at U. of Erlangen, came to Md., 1753/4; Ord. York, Pa., 1755-1756; sett. Brecknock, Pa., Muddy Creek Chh., 1758-1763; Earl, Pa., Chh. at New Holland, 1758-1763; Ephrata, Pa., Bergstrasse Chh., 1758-1763; Frederick, Md., 1763-1768; Antietam, Md., 1763-1768; Brunswick, N. Y., Gilead Chh., 1768-1788; Luth.; d. 1788.

BENEDICT SCHWOPE (Schwob), b. Europe, ca. 1730; sett. Baltimore, 2nd. Chh., 1770-Ord. 1771-1773; Ruling Elder, St. Benjamin's Chh., Westminster, Md., 1763-1770; sett. Westminster, Md., 1773-1776; removed to Eastern Tennessee; German Reformed; d. Md., ca. 1810.

ROBERT SCOTT, b. Kent, Eng., K.B. Md., Mar. 10, 1707/8; arriv. Md., 1708; sett. All Faiths' Parish (St. Mary's) Md., July 1708-1734; Ep.; d. All Faiths' Parish, Md., 1734.

JAMES SCOUGAL, came from the Presbytery of Paisley, Scotland, to Am., 1743; sett. Snow Hill, Md., 1743-1746; The Ferry (Worcester) Md., 1743-1746; Buckingham, Md., Chh. at Berlin, 1743-1746; Old Side Presb.; d. Snow Hill, Md., 1746.

RICHARD SEWALL (See *C.C.Del.*), North Sassafras Parish, Md., June 1, 1697-1723; Shrewbury Parish (Kent) Md., induct. May 20, 1709-1713, Sept, 5, 1723-1724; Wye Mills (Talbot) Md., St. Luke's Chh., 1723-1724; Ep.

GEORGE SHADFORD, b. Scotter, Lindsay, Lincolnshire, Eng., Jan. 19, 1739; arriv. Am., 1773; Baltimore Conference, 1773-1778; also N. Y. C., 1773; Va., 1776; Baltimore, 1777; Kent, Del.; returned to Eng., 1778; Meth., d. Eng., Mar. 11, 1816.

SAMUEL SKIPPON, A.B., b. Ireland; A.B., Trinity Coll., Dublin, 1710; K.B. Md., Apr. 6, 1714; sett. Annapolis, Md., St. Anne's Chh., Nov. 1, 1715-1725; Ep.; d. Annapolis, Md., before July 6, 1725.

JOHN SLEMONS, A.M., b. Chester Co., Pa., of Irish parentage; A.B., Princeton, 1760, A.M.; lic. 1762-1763; sett. Highland (Adams) Pa., Lower Marsh Creek Chh., 1764-Ord. May 23, 1765-1774; Taneytown, Md., 1764-1770; Lower Chanceford, Pa., 1774-1799; Slate Ridge, Pa., 1781-Sept. 1791; Presb.; bur. Piney Creek, Md., June 1814, a. 79.

SAMUEL SLOANE, A.B., b. Pa., ca. 1740; A.B., Princeton, 1761; Ord. England, 1765; K.B. Md., Jan. 2, 1766; sett. St. Paul's

Parish (Kent) Md., curate, 1766-1767; Worcester Parish (Worc.) Md., 1768-1770; Coventry Parish (Somerset) Md., 1770-1785; Ep.; d. Coventry Parish, Md., 1807, a. 67.

BISHOP PETRUS SLUYTER, came to Am., 1679, to find a place for settlement; chose Bohemia Manor, Md., and returned to Holland, 1680; arriv. N. Y. C., July 27, 1683; Bishop at Bohemia Manor, Md., 1684-1722; Labadist; d. Bohemia Manor, Md., 1722.

LAWRENCE STARKEY (alias Sankey), b. Lancaster, England, 1606; adm. S.J., 1636; sett. Port Tobacco (Charles) Md., St. Ignatius' Chh., 1648-1657; R.C.; d. Va., Feb. 19, 1657.

BISHOP JOHN STAUFFER, sett. Beaver Creek (Washington) Md., Mt. Zion Chh., before 1763; Mennonite.

JOHN CONRAD STEINER, SEN., b. Winterthur, Switzerland, Jan. 1, 1707, son of Hon. Jacob and Ursula (Sutzer) Steiner; Mettmenstetten, Switz., vicar, 1726-1728, 1733-1735, St. Peterzell, minister, 1735-1747; also at St. Gall, Hemnurg and St. George, near Wintherthur; came to Philadelphia, Sept. 25, 1749; sett. Philadelphia, Pa., 1749-1751, 1759-1762; Germantown, Pa., 1750-1756; Whitpain, Pa., 1752-1756; sett. as minister of the ffg. chhs. in Md., 1756-1759: Frederick, Antietam, Glade, Middletown, Pipe Creek, and Turkey; Union (Adams) Pa., 1756-1759; Conewago, Pa., 1756-1759; Winchester, Va., 1756-1759; Germ. Reform.; d. Philadelphia, Pa., July 6, 1762, a. 55 yrs. (GS).

JOHN STEPHEN, b. Scotland, 1741; Ord. 1764; K.B. Tobago, Oct. 4, 1764; sett. West Indies, 1764-1765; induct. All Faiths' Parish (St. Mary's) Md., July 4, 1769, sett. All Faith's, Mar. 19, 1765-1784; Ep.; d. All Faiths' Parish, Md., 1784, ae. 43.

JAMES STERLING, A.M., d. Dowrass, Kings Co., Ireland, 1701, son of Capt. James Sterling; A.B., Trinity Coll., Dublin, 1720, A.M., 1733; K.B. Md., Sept. 16, 1737; sett. All Hallows' Parish (Anne Arundel) Md., 1737-1739; Annapolis, Md., St. Anne's Chh., July 18, 1739-May 6, 1740; St. Paul's Parish (Kent) Md., induct. Aug. 26, 1740-1763; regimental chaplain, 1733; author, poet, colonial customs official; Ep.; d. St. Paul's Parish, Md., Nov. 10, 1763.

HUGH STEVENSON (See *C.C.Del.*), Ord. Snow Hill, Md., 1729-1733; Presb.; d. Philadelphia, Pa., May, 1744.

WILLIAM STEWART, b. Great Britain; Ord. June 1719; Princess Anne (Som.) Md., Manokin Chh., 1718-1734; Salisbury (Wicomico) Md., Wicomico Chh., 1718-1734; Rehoboth (Som.) Md., Pocomoke Chh., 1723-1734; Presb.; d. Md., 1734.

FRANCIS STOURTON, b. Devonshire, Eng., son of Francis Stourton; sett. William and Mary Parish (St. Mary's) Md., 1675-1679; St. Mary's City, St. George's Chh., Poplar Hill, 1675-1679; Ep.; d. St. Mary's City, Md., 1679.

JOHN CASPAR STOEVER, SR. (See *C.C.Pa.*), sett. Frederick, Md., 1730-1734; Luth.

WILLIAM STOVER, b. ca. 1725; sett. Antietam (Washington) Md., 1752-1795; Tunker, Dunkard or German Baptist; d. 1795.

ROBERT STRAWBRIDGE, b. Drummer's Nave, near Carrick-on-Shannon, Co. Leitrim, Ireland; came to Am., ca. 1760; New Windsor (Carroll) Md., Sam's Creek Chh., 1760-1775; Baltimore Conference, 1766-1781; Frederick, Md., 1775-1775; farmer at Long Green (Baltimore) Md.; Meth.; d. Long Green, Md., 1781.

THEOPHILUS SWIFT, (perhaps son of Rev. William Swift of Va.), sett. Port Tobacco Parish (Charles) Md., 1750-1762; Durham Parish, Md., 1750-1762; Ep.; d. Port Tobacco Parish, Md., 1762.

MOSES TABBS, A.M., b. Dublin, Ireland, 1718, son of Moses Tabbs; pens. Trinity Coll., Dublin, Feb. 18, 1735/6, a. 18; A.B., 1740, A.M., 1748; sett. Prince George Parish (Montgomery) Md., 1751-1752; William and Mary Parish (St. Mary's) Md., 1752-1776; St. Mary's City, Md., 1752-1776; St. Andrew's Parish (St. Mary's) Md., 1753-1757; Ep.

JACOB TANNER, son of Michael Tanner (Danner or Donner); sett. Codorus (York) Pa., 1758-1770; Monocacy, Md., 1770-1789; Tunker or Germ. Bapt.; living 1789.

NATHANIEL TAYLOR, b. Scotland; Ord. Scotland, 1702-1703; came with his congregation to Md.; sett. Upper Marlborough (Prince George) Md., on the Patuxent River, 1703-1710; Presb.; d. Upper Marlborough, Md., 1710.

CHARLES TENNENT (See *C.C. Del.*), sett. Buckingham (Worcester) Md., at Berlin, Eastern Shore, 1763-1767; Presb.; d. Buckingham, Md., Feb. 25, 1771, ae. 59.

OWEN THOMAS (See *C.C.Del.*), sett. Yellow Springs (Frederick) Md., 1748-1760; Bapt.; d. Vincent, Pa., Nov. 12, 1760, a. 68 (GS).

RICHARD THOMAS, alias Webster, arriv. Md., 1711; S.J., R.C.; d. Jan. 16, 1735.

THOMAS THOMPSON, K.B. Md., Mar. 10, 1710/11; sett. Dorchester Parish (Dorchester) Md., 1712-1736; Ep.; d. Dorchester Parish, Md., 1736.

WILLIAM THOMSON, D.D., b. Pa., May 22, 1735, son of Rev. Samuel Thomson (a Presb. clergyman); D.D., Washington Coll., 1785; Ord. London, Dec. 1759; lic. Dec. 23, 1759; K.B. Pa., Jan. 16, 1760; sett. Huntington, Pa., 1760-1769; York, Pa., 1760-1769; Carlisle, Pa., 1760-1769; Trenton, N. J., St. Michael's Chh., Apr. 1, 1769-Apr. 12, 1773; Lawrence, N. J., Maidenhead Chh., 1769-1773; North Elk Parish (Cecil) Md., May 1, 1773-1781; St. Mary Anne's Parish (Cecil) Md., 1773-1779; North Sassafras Parish (Cecil) Md., 1779-1785; Augustine Parish (Cecil) Md., 1780-1785; Ep.; d. North Sassafras Parish, Md., 1785, ae. 50.

JOHN THORNTON (poss. b. Bridgenorth, Eng., 1701, son of Leonard Thornton; pens. Trinity Coll., Dublin, June 25, 1717, a.

16 ?); sett. Christ Church Parish (Queen Annes) Md., 1753 (and poss. 1746-1765); Ep.

THOMAS THORNTON, b. 1715; K.B. Md., Oct. 10, 1754; lic. Sept. 22, 1754; sett. Port Tobacco Parish (Charles) Md., 1762-1777; King George's Parish (Stafford) Va., 1785-1787; St. George's Parish (Spotsylvania) Va., 1788-1791; Dettingen Parish (Prince William) Va., 1791; Ep.; d. Dumfries (King William) Va., 1791, a. 76.

GEORGE THOROLD, b. Berkshire, Eng., Feb. 11, 1670; arriv. Md., 1700; sett. Newtown (St. Mary's) Md., 1700-1742; Chapel Point (Charles) Md., St. Ignatius' Chh., St. Thomas' Manor, 1700-1742; Superior, 1725-1734; R.C.; d. St. Thomas' Manor, Md., Nov. 15, 1742.

JOSEPH THREKELD (Threlkeld), b. Eng.; Ord. before 1745; sett. Va.; sett. Prince George Parish (Montgomery) Md., 1767-1783; Ep.; d. Rock Creek, Md., 1783.

THOMAS THURSTON, imprisoned in Va. as a Quaker preacher; came to Md. and preached there, 1657, was expelled for this, but returned, 1658, took up land, went into politics, and was disowned by the Friends for his "worldliness"; Friend.

WILLIAM TIBBS, A.B., b. 1674, son of Richard Tibbs of Middleton Stoney, Oxford; matric. Merton Coll., Oxford, Feb. 18, 1691/2, a. 18; A.B., 1698; K.B. Md. May 7, 1701; sett. Baltimore, Md., St. Paul's Chh., 1701-1731 (poss. to 1738); Ep.

EDWARD TIDDER, alias Ingleby, sett. Md., 1663-1667; S.J., R.C.

WILLIAM TOMPSON, A.B. (see *C.C.N.E.*, p. 205), b. Winwick, Lancashire, England, 1598; Brazenose Coll., Oxford; A.B., 1621/2; preached at Winwick; sett. York, Me., 1637-1639; Ord. Quincy, Mass. (1st Chh. in Braintree), Nov. 19, 1639, as first minister; sett. Quincy (1st Chh.), 1639-1666; missionary to Va., 1643; minister of a Puritan Chh., at Annapolis, Md., 1644-1648 (Neill: *Terra Mariae, or Threads of Maryland Colonial History*, 1867, pp. 74-81, q.v.); Congregationalist; d. Quincy (Braintree), Mass., Dec. 10, 1666, ae. 68 yrs. (See also, Frederick Lewis Weis: REVEREND WILLIAM TOMPSON (1598-1666) OF BRAINTREE, MASSACHUSETTS, AND SOME OF HIS DESCENDANTS, Lancaster, 1933, pp. 201, typed *ms.*)

EDWARD TOPP, JR., A.B., b. 1678, son of Rev. Robert Topp of Rochester, Kent; matric. Brasenose Coll., Oxford, Mar. 23, 1692/3, a. 16; A.B., Mar. 18, 1696/7; K.B. Md., Jan. 11, 1697/8; sett. Westminster Parish (formerly Broad Neck Parish, Anne Arundel Co.), Md., 1696-1698; Baltimore, Md., St. Paul's Chh., 1696-1702; Annapolis, Md., St. Anne's Chh., 1704-1706; Ep.

WILLIAM TRAILE, b. 1640, son of Rev. Robert Traile, a Scotch minister; sett. Lifford, Donegal, Ireland; sett. Rehoboth (Somerset) Md., Pocomoke Chh., June 1683-1688; returned to Scotland, 1689/90; sett. Borthwick near Edinburgh, Scotland; Presb.

GEORGE TROTTER (See *C.C.Del.*), sett. Somerset Parish,

Md., 1696-1703; Stepney Parish, Md., 1696-1703; All Faiths' Parish (St. Mary's) Md., 1703-1707; Ep.

GEORGE TUBMAN, A.M., b. 1669, son of Richard Tubman of Talantire, Cumberland; matric. Queen's Coll., Oxford, Mar. 16, 1686/7, a. 18; A.B., 1690, A.M., 1693; came to Md., 1694; sett. Durham Parish (Charles) Md., 1694-1701; William and Mary Parish (Charles) Md., 1695-1700; Port Tobacco Parish (Charles) Md., 1694-1701; Piscataway Parish (Prince George) Md., 1696-1701; Ep.; d. Piscataway Parish, Md., ca. 1701.

JOHN TURLING, sett. Durham Parish, Md., 1684-(1690); St. Paul's Parish (Prince George) Md., 1691-(1694); Christ Church Parish (Calvert) Md., ca. 1691; All Faiths' Parish, Md., 1691-(1694); Ep.

PETER TUSTIAN, A.M., b. Warwickshire, England, 1696, son of Peter Tustian of Hartwick; matric. Christ Coll., Oxford, May 5, 1710, a. 14; A.B., Feb. 18, 1713/4, A.M.; KB. S. C., Nov. 4, 1719; sett. St. George's Parish, Dorchester, S. C., 1719-1721; St. James' Parish (Anne Arundel) Md., 1721-1736; Ep.

JOHN URMSTONE (Urmstons), curate, Eastham, Essex, England, 1706-1709; S.P.G. missionary, N. C., Edenton (Chowan) N. C., St. Paul's Chh., 1709-1720; St. John's Parish (Pasquotank) N. C., 1709-1720; K.B. Va., June 29, 1722; poss. Philadelphia, Pa., Christ Chh., 1723; Shrewsbury Parish (Kent) Md., 1724-1731; North Sassafras Parish (Cecil) Md., 1724-1731; Ep.; "Burned to death in N. C.," 1732.

JOHN URQUAHART, K.B. Md., Feb. 6, 1732/3; sett. All Faiths' Parish, Md., Nov. 11, 1734-Feb. 17, 1764; St. Andrew's Parish (St. Mary's) Md., 1744-1764; Ep.; d. All Faiths' Parish (St. Mary's) Md., Feb. 17, 1764.

RICHARD UTLEY (See *C.C.Del.*), sett. Graceham, Md., 1752-1755, 1770-1771; Moravian; d. Salem, N. C., Oct. 9, 1775.

LAURENTIUS VAN DEN BOSCH (See *C.C.N.E.*), Leyden U., 1679; sett. Kingston, N. Y., June 20, 1687-Oct. 1689; Staten Island, N. Y., South Side Huguenot Chh., 1687-1689 (1686-1687?); North Sassafras Parish (Cecil) Md., 1692-1696; Shrewsbury Parish (Cecil) Md., 1692-1696; St. Paul's Parish (Kent) Md., 1693-1696; Fr. Ref., Huguenot, Dutch Ref., Ep.; d. St. Paul's Parish, Md., 1696.

Father WALDEGRAVE, alias Pelham, S.J., R.C.; came to Md., 1674.

PHILIP WALKER, lic. Mar. 25, 1756; K.B. Md., Apr. 8, 1756; sett. St. Mary's Whitechapel Parish (Caroline) Md., 1756-1767; Ep.

GEORGE FREDERICK WALLAUER, b. Appenheim, near Bingen, where his father was the minister; matric. Marburg, Apr. 22, 1763; came from Europe, 1771; sett. Baltimore, Md., 1st Germ. Ref. Chh., 1772-May 2, 1776; Germ. Ref.; joined the British army and returned to Europe.

JAMES WALTON, sett. Frederick, Md., 1765-1768; Newtown, 1769; R.C.

WILLIAM WAPPELER, arr. Md., 1742; sett. Newtown, 1742-1748; ret. to Europe, 1748; R.C.; d. Ghent, 1781.

HENRY WARREN, sett. Newtown (St. Mary's) Md., 1668-1668; R.C.; d. England, June 7, 1702.

WILLIAM WARREN (alias Pelham), Md., 1669-1671; R.C.; d. Md., Feb. 7, 1671.

WILLIAM WATTERS, b. Baltimore Co., Md., Oct. 16, 1751; Baltimore Conference, 1773-1833; sett. Chester Circuit, Pa., 1774-1774; Frederick, Md., 1775-1775; Meth.; d. 1833.

RICHARD WEBSTER, Eastern Shore, Md., Dec. 24, 1772; Chester Circuit, Pa., 1775; Benson's Chapel, Uwchlan, Pa., 1775; Goshen, Pa., 1775; West Whiteland, 1775; Madison St. Chh., Chester, Pa., 1775; Meth.

WILLIAM WEST, D.D., b. Fairfax Co., Va., 1739; William and Mary Coll., 1756-1760; D.D., Washington Coll., Kent Co., Md., 1785; Ord. London, Nov. 24, 1761; K.B. Va., Nov. 28, 1761; sett. Westminster Parish (Anne Arundel) Md., St. Margaret's, 1763-1767; St. Andrew's Parish (St. Mary's) Md., Leonardstown, Nov. 17, 1763-1772; St. George's Parish (Harford) Md., Perrymans, 1772-1779; St. Paul's Parish (Baltimore) Md., June 7, 1779-1790; Ep.; d. St. Paul's Parish, Md., Mar. 30, 1791, ae. 52.

ROBERT WEYMAN, b. 1694, son of William Weyman of Pembroke; matric. Jesus Coll., Oxford, Mar. 3, 1713/4, a. 19; K.B. Pa., Oct. 1, 1719; arriv. Pa., Nov. 16, 1719; sett. Newtown, Pa., Radnor, Dec. 1719-1730, S.P.G.; Oxford, Pa., 1719-1728; Caernarvon, Pa., 1719-1728; Frankford, Pa., 1719-1728; Whitemarsh, Pa., 1719-1730; St. George's Parish (Harford) Md., 1722-1724; Upper Providence, Pa., 1723-1730; Burlington, N. J., 1728-1737; Bristol, Pa., 1730-1737; Ep.; d. Burlington, N. J., Nov. 28, 1737.

JACOB WEYMER, b. Germany, 1734, came Am., 1751; schoolmaster, catechist and preacher, 1751-1768; Ord. 1770; sett. Albany, N. Y., 1770-1770; Greenwich, Pa., 1770-1770; Heidelberg, Pa., 1770-1770; Lowhill, Pa., 1770-1770; Lynn, Pa., at Jacob's Chh., Ebenezer or Organ Chh., and Tresbackers Chh., 1770-1770; Washington, Pa., 1773-1786; Chambersburg (Franklin) Pa., 1784-1790; and the ffg. chhs. in Md. from Sept. 1770-1790; Cavetown, Conococheague, Funkstown, Hagerstown, Mechanicstown and Troxel's Chh.; German Reformed; d. Hagerstown, Md., May 12, 1790.

ANDREW WHITE, b. London, England, ca. 1579; educ. at English Coll., Seville, Spain; Douai Coll., France; St. Alban's Coll., Valladolid, 1595; Ord. Douai, France, 1605; banished from England, 1606; adm. S.J., Louvain, Feb. 2, 1609; missionary in England, 1609-1619; came to Md. with Lord Baltimore, 1633; sett. St. Mary's City, Md., Mar. 25, 1633/4-1644, 1648-1653; taken in chains to England, 1644; imprisoned in London; escaped; returned to Md., 1648-1653; sett. Port Tobacco (Charles) Md., 1641-1644, 1648-1653; Patuxent,

Md., 1648-1653; R.C.; called the "Apostle to Maryland, 1634"; returned to Eng., 1653; d. London, England, Dec. 27, 1656.

JONATHAN WHITE (A.B., Jesus Coll., Cambridge, 1680/1, A.M.; vicar at Youlgreave, Co. Derby, 1685 ?), sett. William and Mary Parish (Charles) Md., 1700-1708; All Faiths' Parish (St. Mary's) Md., 1707-1708; Queen Anne's Parish (Prince George) Md., 1708-1717; Ep.

HENRY WHITENHALL, arriv. Md., 1724; sett. Anne Arundel Co., Md., 1733-1734; S.J., R.C.; d. England, May 27, 1745.

JAMES WHITGREAVE, arriv. Md., Dec. 1724; sett. Anne Arundel Co., Md., 1733-1737; S.J., R.C.

ABRAHAM WHITWORTH, sett. Kent County, Md., 1774; expelled for bad conduct; Meth.

POLYCARP WICKSTED, arriv. Md., 1674; sett. Newport (Charles) Md., 1674-1674; Franciscan; R.C.

CHARLES FREDERICK WILDBAHN, educ. at U. of Halle; schoolteacher at Winchester, Va.; lic. 1762; sett. West Manheim, Pa., 1751-1752; Union (Adams) Pa., 1763-1782; Hanover, Pa (and Conewago), 1765-1782; Frederick, Md., 1768-1770, 1796-1799; Conococheague, Md., 1770-1782; Hagerstown, Md., 1770-1771; Taneytown, Md., 1770-1782; Reading, Pa., 1782-1796; also at Codorus, Pa., Owen's Creek, Point Creek and Thomas Creek, time unknown; Luth.; d. 1804.

COMMISSARY CHRISTOPHER WILKINSON, K.B. Md., Feb. 24, 1710/11 (as Williamson); sett. All Hallows' Parish (Worcester) Md., 1710-1713; St. Paul's Parish (Queen Annes) Md., Centerville, 1713-1729; Commissary, Md., 1716-1729; Ep.; d. Talbot, Md., Apr. 15, 1729.

STEPHEN WILKINSON, K.B. Md., Jan. 24, 1725/6; sett. St. George's Parish (Harford) Md., June 4, 1726-1744; Ep.; d. St. George's Parish, Md., Mar. 25, 1744.

WILLIAM WILKINSON, A.B. (prob. of Cheshire, b. 1603; matric. Brasenose Coll., Oxford, Nov. 2, 1621, a. 18; A.B., Oct. 26, 1624); came Md., 1650; sett. King and Queen Parish (St. Mary's) Md., Chaptico, 1650-1663; St. Mary's City, Md., St. George's Chh., Poplar Hill, 1650-1663; William and Mary Parish, Md., 1650-1663; Ep.; will made May 29, 1663; d. King and Queen Parish, Md., Aug. 1663.

JOHN WILLIAMS, b. Flintshire, Wales; sett. Fredericktown, Md., 1763-1763; ret. to England, 1768; R.C.

ALEXANDER WILLIAMSON, lic. Bsp. London, 1711; K.B. Md., Oct. 10, 1710; sett. St. Paul's Parish (Kent) Md., Apr. 10, 1711-1725; Ep.

ALEXANDER WILLIAMSON, b. All Saints' (Calvert) Md., ca. 1727, son of Rev. James Williamson; Ord. London, 1755; K.B. Md., Apr. 8, 1756; St. Andrew's Parish (St. Mary's) Md., Leonardstown, 1757-1761; curate, Annapolis, Md., Apr. 1759-1761; Prince George Parish (Montgomery) Md., Feb. 1761-1776; Christ Church Parish (Calvert) Md., 1767-1768; Rock Creek Parish, Md. (now Washington, D. C.), 1761-1776; Ep.; d. Georgetown, D. C., a. ca. 60.

JAMES WILLIAMSON, b. Scotland; K.B. Md., Jan. 21, 1712/3; induct. Shrewsbury Parish (Kent) Md., 1713-1722; All Saints' Parish (Calvert) Md., May 11, 1722-1724; Ep.

THOMAS WILSON, sett. Killybegs, Donegal, Ireland, Aug. 1676-1681; came to Somerset Co., Md., Jan. 1685; sett. Princess Anne, Md., Manokin Chh., 1685-1702; will proved, Jan. 18, 1702/3; Presb.; d. Princess Anne, Md., 1702.

JOHN WOOD, sett. Md., 1636-1638; S.J., R.C.

WILLIAM WOOD, sett. in Md., 1700-1711; S.J., R.C.; d. Aug. 1720.

JAMES WOOTTON, K.B. Md., Aug. 12, 1703; sett. Annapolis, Md., 1706-1710; Westminster Parish (Anne Arundel) Md., 1705-1710; Ep.

RICHARD WRIGHT, lic. 1770; came to Am., 1772; itinerant min. in Md. and Va.; Norfolk, Va., 1773-1774; Meth.

WILLIAM WYE, A.B., b. Co. Louth, Ireland, 1684, son of Rev. Mossom Wye; pens. Trinity Coll., Dublin, Aug. 27, 1701, a. 17; A.B., 1706; K.B. S. C., Aug. 9, 1717; S.P.G. missionary, Goose Creek, S. C., Aug. 1717-Dec. 1717; sett. St. Stephen's Parish (Northumberland) Va., 1727-1731; Coventry Parish, Md., 1731-1736; North Elk Parish (Cecil) Md., Oct. 16, 1736-1744; Ep.; d. North Elk Parish, Md., Nov. 16, 1744.

JOHN YEO, A.B. (See *C.C.Del.*), sett. Christ Chh. Parish (Calvert Md., 1675-1678; All Faiths' Parish (St. Mary's) Md., 1675-1678; St. John's Parish (Baltimore) Md., 1683-1686; St. George's Parish (Harford) Md., 1683-1686; Ep.; d. St. John's Parish (Baltimore) Md., 1686.

JOHANN MICHAEL ZAHM (alias Toll), b. Sunzheim, Rheinish-Bavaria; Ord. Dec. 1758; sett. Graceham, Md., Oct. 6, 1758-1762; minister in rural churches; school teacher; Treas. of the Fund for the Support of the Ministry of the Moravian Chh., 1780-1787; d. Bethlehem, Pa., Dec. 1787.

NATHANIEL WHITAKER, A.M., A.B., Harvard Coll., 1730, A.M.; went to England for ordination; K.B. Md., Feb. 4, 1741/2; for the lurid career of Mr. Whitaker as an Ep. clergyman in Md., see the forthcoming volume of Clifford K. Shipton: *Sibley's Harvard Graduates*, Vol. VIII.

THE COLONIAL CLERGY OF DELAWARE, 1638-1776

PROVOST ISRAEL ACRELIUS, b. Oster-aker, Sweden, Dec. 4, 1714, son of Rev. John and Sara (Gahm) Acrelius; Univ. of Upsala, 1727-1743; Ord. 1743; domestic chaplain, 1743-1745; minister at Riala, Kulla and Norra Ljustero, Sweden, 1745-1749; arrived, Delaware, Nov. 1749; Provost of the Swedish Lutheran Churches in America, Nov. 6, 1749-Nov. 9, 1756; sett. Wilmington, Del. (Old Swedes Chh.), Nov. 6, 1749-Nov. 9, 1756; Chester, Pa. (S.L. Chh. at Upland—the oldest church in Pa.), 1749-1756; Chester, Pa. (St. Paul's Chh., Ep.), 1755-1756; Marcus Hook, Pa. (St. Martin's Chh., Ep.), 1751-1756; Penn, Pa. (St. John's Chh., Ep.), 1751-1755; returned to Sweden, Nov. 9, 1756; sett. Dean of Fellingsbro, Sweden, 1756-1800; author of *History of New Sweden*, 1759; Swedish Lutheran; d. Fellingsbro, Sweden, Apr. 25, 1800.

ALEXANDER ADAMS, b. Eng., ca. 1680; Ord. (Bp. London), 1703; K.B. to Md., Aug. 27, 1703; miss. V.S.P.G.F.P.; sett. Laurel, Del. (Christ Chh., Broad Creek Chh., Little Creek), 1704-1764; Somerset Parish, Md. (Chhs. at Princess Anne and Monie), 1704-1769; Stepney Parish, Md., 1704-1769; Ep., d. Stepney Parish, Md., 1769, a. ca. 91.

HECTOR ALISON, A.M., A.M. (Hon.), U. Pa., 1759; Ord. White Clay Creek, Del., New Side Chh., 1746; sett. White Clay Creek, 1745-1753; Appoquinimink, Del., 1746-1749; Drawyer's Creek, Del., 1753-1758; Chaplain, 2nd Batt., Pa. militia, 1759; Presb.

JAMES ANDERSON, b. Edinburgh, Scotland, Nov. 17, 1678; Ord. Irvine Presbytery (Scotland), Nov. 17, 1708; arr. in Am., Apr. 22, 1709; sett. Rappahannock, Va., Apr. 1709-1710; New Castle, Del. (1st Chh.), 1710-1716/7; New York, N. Y. (1st Presb. Chh., Old Side), Sept. 24, 1717-1726; East Donegal, Pa., inst. Aug. 1727, sett. 1726-1740; Derry, Pa., 1729-1732; Swatara, Pa., Paxton Chh. on Fishing Creek, 1729-1732; Presb.; d. Marietta, Donegal (Lancaster), Pa., July 16, 1740.

JOHN ANDREWS, D.D., b. near Head of Elk, Cecil Co., Md., Apr. 1, 1746, son of Moses and Letitia Andrews; A.B., U. Pa., 1766, A.M., 1767; D.D., Washington Coll., Md., 1785; Ord. London, Eng., Feb. 15, 1767; K.B., Pa., Feb. 24, 1767; sett. Lewes, Del., St. Peter's Chh., 1767-1769; Broadkill, Del., St. John Baptist Chh., 1767-1769; Cedar Creek Hundred, Del., St. Matthew's Chh., 1767-1769; Dagsboro, Del., St. George's Chh., 1767-1769; Indian River, Del., 1767-1769; York, Pa., St. John's Chh., 1769-1772; Carlisle, Pa., St. John's Chh., 1769-1772; Huntington, Pa., Chh. at York Springs, 1769-1772;

Rector, St. John's Parish (Caroline) Md., 1772-1776; Rector, York, Pa., St. John's Chh., 1776-1782; Rector, St. Thomas' Parish (Baltimore) Md., Apr. 13, 1782-1785; Vice-Provost, U. Pa., 1789-1810; Provost, 1810-1813; Am. Pil. Soc., 1786; Ep.; d. Philadelphia, Pa., Mar. 29, 1813, ae. 67.

THOMAS BARTON, A.M., b. Co. Monaghan, Ireland, 1730; Trinity Coll., Dublin; came to Am., 1750; A.M. (hon) U. Pa., 1760, A.M. (hon) Columbia, 1770; Ord. (Bsp. London), Jan. 29, 1755; K.B., Pa., Feb. 7, 1755; arr. Pa., Apr. 10, 1755; sett. York, Pa., May 1755-1765; Carlisle, Pa., 1755-1758; Huntington, Pa., 1755-1758; Caernarvon, Pa., Bangor Chh. at Churchtown, 1759-1776; Salisbury, St. John's Chh. at Compassville and West Caln, Pa., 1759-1776; Rector, Lancaster, Pa., St. James's Chh., 1760-1778; Mill Creek, Del., St. James's Chh. at Stanton, 1760-1780; Penn, Pa., St. John's Chh., 1760-1780; Rector, Caernarvon, Pa., St. Thomas' Chh. at Marytown, 1765-1780; Chaplain, Fr. and Ind. War, 1758; Tory in Rev., escaped to N. Y., 1776, but returned; S.P.G., Ep., d. N. Y. City, May 25, 1780, ae. 50.

WILLIAM BECKET, b. Over Peover, Cheshire, Eng., Apr. 25, 1697, son of John and Mary Becket; K.B., Pa., Mar. 25, 1721; arr. Lewes, Del., Sept. 1, 1721; sett. Lewes, Del., St. Peter's Chh., 1721-1743; Cedar Creek Hundred, Del., St. Matthew's Chh., 1721-1743; Dagsboro, Del., Prince George's Chapel, 1721-1743; Broadkill, Del., St. John Baptist Chh., 1728-1743; Indian River, Del., St. George's Chapel, 1728-1743; S.P.G., Ep., d. Lewes, Del., Aug. 20, 1743.

WILLIAM BLACK, b. Dumfries, Scotland, ca. 1679; K.B., N. J., Sept. 5, 1706; S.P.G. Missionary to Sussex Co., Del., 1708-1709; sett. Lewes, Del., St. Peter's Chh., July 26, 1708-May 1709; Cedar Creek Hundred, Del., 1708-1709; Accomac Parish, Va., 1709/10-1724; Ep.

THOMAS BLUETT (sometimes given as Blewer), S.P.G. missionary to Kent Co. Del.; sett. North Farnham Parish (Richmond) Va., 1739-1742; Dover, Del., Christ Chh., 1745-1749; Milford, Del., Christ Chh., 1745-1749; Mispillion, Del., Christ Chh., 1745-1749; Ep., d. Dover, Del., Jan. 25, 1749.

PROVOST ERICK TOBIAS BJORK, Ord. Upsala; arrived in Philadelphia from Westmanland, Sweden, June 30, 1697; sett. Wilmington (New Castle) Del., Old Swedes Chh., 1697-1714; left June 29, 1714; Chester, Pa., Chh. at Upland, 1697-1714; Crane Hook, Del., Chh. at Tran Hook, Dec. 1697-1699; Provost of all Swedish Lutheran Churches in America, 1713-1714; returned to Sweden, 1714; sett. Fahlun, Dalcarlia, Sweden, 1714-1740; d. Fahlun, Sweden, Aug. 21, 1740.

BISHOP JOHN PETER BOEHLER, b. Frankfort a/M., Germany, Dec. 3, 1712, son of John Conrad and Antoinette Elisabetha (Hanf) Boehler; Univ. of Jena, 1731-1736; Ord. Herrenhut, Saxony, Germany, Dec. 1737; arriv. at Savannah, Ga., Oct. 15, 1738; sett.

THE COLONIAL CLERGY OF DELAWARE 73

Savannah, Ga., Oct. 1738-Jan. 1739; Purysburg, S. C., 1738-1739; Nazareth, Pa., 1740-1741; returned to Europe, Jan. 29, 1740/1-1742; 2nd visit to Am., arr. Philadelphia, June 7, 1742; Bethlehem, Pa., 1742-1745; Philadelphia, 1743-1745; preached at the following places, 1743-1745: Burlington, N. J., Cranbury, N. J., Dover, Del.; Duck Creek, Del.; Durham, Pa.; Lawrence, N. J.; Lewes, Del.; Lower Salford, Pa.; Manatawny, Pa.; Middletown, N. J.; Southampton, Neshaminy Chh.; Swedish Settlements, N. J.; Trenton, N. J.; Upper Providence, Pa., at Trappe; returned to Europe, Apr. 8, 1745; consecrated Bsp. for America at Marienborn, Germany, Jan. 10, 1748; returned to Am., Sept. 13, 1753-Aug. 28, 1755; at Bethlehem, Pa., Dec. 16, 1756-1764; final departure for Europe, May 7, 1764; next to Spangenberg, the most eminent leader of the Moravians in America; President, Pa. Synod; d. London, England, Apr. 27, 1775.

PROVOST ANDREW BORELL, sett. Wilmington, Del., Old Swedes' Chh., 1759-1768; Chester, Pa., Chh. at Upland, 1759-1768; Provost of the Swedish Lutheran Churches of America, 1759-1768; d. Wilmington, Del., Apr. 5, 1768.

SAMUEL BROOK, b. Prince George Co., Md.; Ord. 1754; Missionary, S.P.G., Del. 1754-1756; sett. St. George's Parish (Harford) Md., 1754; New Castle, Del., Immanuel Chh., 1754-1756; Ep.; d. New Castle, Del., Oct. 25, 1756.

ALEXANDER CAMPBELL, K.B. for Va., Dec. 30, 1725; S.P.G. Missionary at Appoquinimink, Del., 1726-1729; Middletown, Del., St. Anne's Chh., 1726-1729; Setauket, L. I., N. Y., Caroline Chh. 1729-1732; Ep.

BENJAMIN CAMPBELL, came from Ireland; adm. New Castle Presbytery, Nov. 5, 1729; Ord. New Castle Presby. before Sept. 1733; sett. New Castle, Del. (1st Chh.), 1729-1734; Presb.; d. New Castle, Del., Oct. 1734.

JOHN CAMPANIUS, b. Stockholm, Sweden, Aug. 15, 1601, son of John Peter Campanius; Univ. Upsala; Ord. July 19, 1633; preceptor of the orphan's seminary in Stockholm; arr. at Fort Christiana on the Delaware, Feb. 15, 1642/3; sett. Wilmington, Del., Old Swedes' Chh., 1643-1648; Tinicum, Pa., New Goeteborg Chh., 1643-1648; New Castle, Del., (1st Chh.), 1643-1648; Chester, Pa., Upland Chh., 1643-1648; returned to Sweden, May 16, 1648; Chaplain to the Admiralty; Rector at Frosthuelt and Hernevi, Sweden, 1648-1683; Sw. Luth.; d. Stockholm, Sweden, Sept. 17, 1683.

CASPARUS CARPENTIER, prob. son of the Rev. Casper Carpentier; minister at Amersfoort, Holland, 1650, at Amsterdam, 1650; arr. in Am., 1657; sett. New Castle, Del. (1st Chh.), 1657-1684; also supplied the French Reformed Chh. at New York, N. Y. 1657-1684; Dutch Ref., Fr. Ref.; d. New Castle, Del., 1684.

ROBERT CATHCART, b. Ireland; received and Ord. New Castle Presbytery, Apr. 15, 1730; sett. Brandwine Manor, Del., 1730-

1754 (Christiana Hundred); Middletown, Pa., 1730-1754; Wilmington, Del., 1740-1754; Presb.; d. Wilmington, Del., 1754.

AARON CLEAVELAND, A.M., H. C., 1735 (See *Col. Clergy N. E.*, p. 58); K.B., Pa., July 30, 1755; sett. Lewes, Del., Halifax, Nova Scota, and New Castle, Del., 1755-1757; Ep.; d. Philadelphia, Pa., Aug. 11, 1757, ae. 41.

JOHN CLUBB, b. Wales; K.B., Pa., Apr. 3, 1704; Philadelphia, Pa., schoolmaster and asst. at Christ Church, 1704-1708; Oxford, Pa., Trinity Chh., 1708-1710, 1714-1715; Appoquinimink, Del., 1712-1713; Middletown, Del., 1712-1713; Newtown, Pa., St. David's Chh. at Radnor, Sept. 1714-Dec. 1715; Ep.; d. Radnor, Pa., Dec. 25, 1715.

THOMAS CRAIGHEAD, A.M., (See *C. C. N. E.*, p. 64); Mill Creek, Del., Chh. at White Clay Creek, inst. Sept. 22, 1724-1731; Brandywine, Del. 1724-1730; Salisbury, Pa., Pequea Chh., inst. Oct. 1733-Sept. 7, 1736; Newville, Pa., Hopewell Chh. at Big Spring, 1737, inst. Oct. 1738-1739; Southampton, Pa., Middle Spring Chh., Nov. 17, 1737-1739; Letterkenney (Franklin) Pa., Rock Spring Chh., 1738-1739; physician; Moderator, Presb. Synod, 1726; d. Newville, Pa., June, 1739.

THOMAS CRAWFORD, b. Scotland; K.B., Md., Jan. 18, 1703/4; sett. Lewes, Del., St. Peter's Chh., 1704-1705; Dover, Del., Christ Chh., 1705-1709; recalled by S.P.G.; Ep.

ROBERT CROSS, b. near Ballykelly, Ireland, 1689; educated in Ireland; came to Am. 1717; Ord. New Castle, Del., Sept. 19, 1719; sett. New Castle, 1st Chh., 1718-May 1722; Jamaica, L. I., N. Y., 1st Chh., Cong.-Presb., Oct. 10, 1723-May 1737; Philadelphia, Pa., 1st Presb. Chh., inst. Nov. 10, 1737-June 22, 1758; leader of the Old Side Presbyterians; d. Philadelphia, Pa., Aug. 9, 1766, s.p. (GS).

DAVID DAVIS, b. Whitechurch, Pembroke, Wales, 1708; came to Am., 1710; Ord. Welsh Tract Baptist Church, 1734; sett. Pencader Hundred, Del., Welsh Tract Chh., 1734-inst. May 27, 1748-1769; Bapt., d. Welsh Tract, Del., Aug. 19, 1769.

JOHN DAVIS A.M., (See *C. C. N. E.*), sett. Welsh Tract, Del., 1769-1770; Bapt.; d. near Wheeling, W. Va., Dec. 13, 1772.

SAMUEL DAVIS, came from Ireland; liv. Somerset Co., Md., Feb. 26, 1684/5; Ord. New Castle, Del., 1705; sett. Snow Hill, Md., 1686-1698, 1718-1725; Lewes, Del., 1691-1715; New Castle, Del., 1691-1717; physician; Presb.; d. Snow Hill, Md., 1725, (inventory taken, Apr. 1725).

WILLIAM DAVIS, b. Castellneth, Glamorganshire, Wales, 1695; came to Am., 1722; returned to Great Britain; again in Vincent, Pa., 1737; sett. Rockhill, Pa., 1749-1768; New Britain, Pa., 1749-1768; sett. Kenton, Del., Old Dutch Creek or Bryn Zion Chh., 1766-1768; Bapt.; d. Dutch Creek, Del., Oct. 3, 1768.

JOHN DICK, b. prob. at West Nottingham, Md.; Ord. West Nottingham, Md., Nov. 12, 1746; sett. Appoquinimink, Del., (New

Side Chh.), 1746-1746; Drawyer's Creek, Del., 1746-1747; New Castle, Del., 1746-1747; Presb.; d. Del., 1747.

SAMUEL EAKIN, A.M., A.B., Princeton, 1763, A.M.; sett. Salem, N. J., 1774-1776; Pencader Hundred, Del., 1776-1783; Chaplain, Rev. War, N. J. Militia; Presb.; d. Pencader, Del., 1784.

JOHN ENEBERG, b. Sweden, 1689; stud. at Upsala; Ord. England, 1729; sett. Philadelphia, Pa. (Gloria Dei or Wicacoa Chh.), 1729-1733; Chester, Pa., Chh. at Upland, 1732-1742; Wilmington, Del., Old Swedes' Chh., 1732-1742; Sw. Luth.; returned to Sweden, 1742.

DAVID EVANS, A.M., b. Wales, ca. 1690, son of Elder David Evans, Esq., of Welsh Tract; came to Am., 1701; A.B., Y.C., 1713, A.M.; Ord. Welsh Tract Chh. (Pencader Hundred), Del., Nov. 3, 1714; sett. Pencader Hundred, Del., 1714-1720; Newark (New Castle) Del., 1714-1720; Tredyffryn, Pa., Old Side Chh. at Great Valley; Sadsbury, Pa., Chh. at Upper Octoraro, 1720-1723; Norriton, Pa., 1727-1731; Pilesgrove, N. J., Apr. 30, 1741-1751; Penns Neck, N. J., Chh. at Quihawken, 1741-1751; Presb. o.s.; d. Pilesgrove, N. J., Feb. 4, 1750/1.

JOEL EVANS, A.B., b. Great Valley Pa., son of Rev. David and Ann Evans; A.B., Y.C., 1740; lic. to preach, Sept. 17, 1741; sett. Deerfield, N. J., 1741-1742; Woodbury (Gloucester) N. J., 1741-1742; Appoquinimink, Del., Apr. 1742-Apr. 1743; Presb., d. Appoquinimink, Del., Apr. 1743.

THOMAS EVANS, came from Caermarthen, Wales; received, New Castle Presbytery, Sept. 14, 1719, licensed, May 28, 1728; Ord. Pencader, Del., May 9, 1723; sett. Pencader Hundred, 1723-1743; Duck Creek, Del., 1723-1743; Newark, Del., 1723-1743; principal of an Old Side academy at Pencader; Presb., d. Pencader, Del., 1743, unm.

JACOB FABRITIUS, a German or Pole, studied at Altdorf; Ord. Grosglogau, Silesia, ca. 1669; sett. New York, N. Y., Holy Trinity Luth. Chh., 1669-1671; Chester, Pa., Chh. at Upland, 1671-1677; Ord. Philadelphia, Pa., Gloria Dei or Wicacoa Sw. Luth. Chh., Trinity Sunday, 1677-1693; Tinicum, Pa., 1677-1677; Wilmington, Del., Old Swedes' Chh., 1677-1691; Crane Hook, Del., Chh. at Tran Hook, 1688-1691; preached in Dutch and Swedish; Luth. and Sw. Luth.; d. Philadelphia, Pa., 1693.

GEORGE FRAZIER, (or Frazer, Fraser, poss. son of Rev. John Fraser), K.B., Pa., Feb. 6, 1732/3; sett. Dover, Del. Christ Church, 1733-1735, S.P.G.; if same as following, he resided for a time at Overwharton Parish, Va. before going to England for ordination; K.B., Va., Aug. 20, 1738; sett. Dale Parish, Va., 1738-1758; Ep.

PHILIP GATCH, b. near Baltimore, Md., Mar. 2, 1751, son of George Gatch; rode Methodist circuit, 1773-1788, in New Jersey, Delaware and Maryland; 1788-1797, in Virginia; sett. Frederick, Md., 1774-1774; went to Ohio in 1797; became associate judge of the

Court of Common Pleas in Ohio, 1803-1824; Meth.; d. Clermont Co., Ohio, December 25, 1835.

GEORGE GILLESPIE, b. Glasgow, Scotland, 1683; educated at the Univ. of Glasgow; lic. Glasgow, Scotland, 1712; came to Am. 1712; Ord. Head of Christiana Chh., White Clay Creek Hundred, Del., May 23, 1713; sett. Head of Christiana, 1713-1760; Lower Brandywine, Del., 1713-1760; White Clay Creek, Del., 1713-1760; Red Clay Creek, Del., 1713-1760; Elk River, Del., 1721-1760; Presb.; d. White Clay Creek, Del., Jan. 2, 1760, ae. 77.

PROVOST LAWRENCE GIRELIUS, arriv. at Wilmington, Del., Oct. 21, 1767; sett. Wilmington, Del., Old Swedes' Chh., 1767-1791; Chester, Pa., Church at Upland, 1767-1791; Provost of the Swedish Lutheran Churches in America, 1767-1791.

TIMOTHY GRIFFITH, b. Great Valley, Pa., son of Elder Timothy Griffith; Y.C., 1742; Ord. Pencader Hundred, Del., 1743; sett. Pencader, 1743-1754; Newark, Del., 1743-1748; missionary in Virginia, 1751; Capt. of the New Castle County Troops, Sept. 1748; res. on a farm at Appoquinimink, Del., 1748-1754; Presb.; d. Appoquinimink, Del., before May, 1754.

THOMAS GRIFFITHS, b. Lanvernach Parish, Pembroke, Wales, 1645; Ord. Wales; arr. Philadelphia, Sept. 8, 1701; sett. Pencader Hundred, Del., Welsh Tract Baptist Chh., 1703-1725; Bapt.; d. Pennepak, Pa., July 25, 1725.

WALTER HACKETT, K.B., Pa., Mar. 4, 1728/9; sett. Middletown (New Castle) Del., St. Anne's Chh., 1729-1733; Appoquinimink, Del., St. Anne's Chh., 1729-1733; North Elk Parish (Cecil) Md., St. Mary Anne's Chh., 1733-1735; Ep.; d. North Elk Parish, Md., 1735.

WARNERUS HADSON, Ord. in Holland for New Castle, Del., 1662, but died on the passage over, 1664; Dutch Reformed.

JOHN HARRIS, A.B., b. Eastern Shore, Md., Sept. 29, 1725, of Welsh parents; A.B., Princeton, 1753; lic. Oct. 12, 1753; Ord. Indian River, Del., 1756-1769; Salisbury, Md., Wicomico Chh., 1756-1764; Princess Anne, Md., Manokin Chh., 1756-1764; sett. Ninety-Six (Abbeville) S. C.; Long Canes, S. C., 1772-Nov. 1779; Boonsborough, S. C., Long Canes Creek Chh., 1772-1779; Bulltown, S. C., 1772-1779; Greenville, S. C., Saluda Chh., 1772-1773; physician; membr. S. C. Prov. Cong.; Old Side Presb.; d. 1790.

COMMISSARY JACOB HENDERSON, b. Glenavy, Ireland, ca. 1685; ed. at Univ. of Glasgow; Ord. (Bsp. of London), June 5, 1710; K.B. Va., July 1, 1710; missionary, S.P.G.; sett. Dover, Del., Christ Church, 1710-1711; New Castle, Del., Immanuel Chh., July 24, 1712-1714; Annapolis, Md., St. Anne's Chh., induct., Apr. 13, 1714; sett. Annapolis (Anne Arundel), Md., 1713-1714; St. Paul's Parish Md., 1714-1717; Leeland, Md., Queen Anne's Parish (Prince George), St. Barnabas's Chh., 1717-1751; Bishop's Commissary for

Md., 1716-1723, 1729-1734; bequeathed £1,000 to the V.S.P.G.F.P.; Ep.; d. Queen Anne's Parish, Md., Aug. 27, 1751, ae. 65.

MATTHEW HENDERSON, b. Fifeshire, Scotland, 1735; educated at Glasgow Univ.; Ord. Scotland, 1758; sett. Pencader (New Castle) Del., Associate Presb. Chh., 1758-1775; Oxford, Pa., Asso. Presb. Chh., 1758-1775; sett. Chartiers and Buffalo (both Washington Co.), Pa., 1782; also at Mingo and Mill Creek, Pa.; Associate Presb.; d. Washington Co., Pa., Oct. 2, 1795, ae. 60.

HUGH HENRY, A.B., A.B., Princeton, 1748; Ord. Rehoboth, Md. (1st Presb. Chh. in Am. at Pocomoke), 1751; sett. Rehoboth, Md., 1751-1763; Salisbury, Md., Wicomico Chh., 1751-1763; Princess Anne (Somerset) Md., Manokin Chh., 1751-1763; Laurel, Del., 1751-1756; New Side Presb.; d. Rehoboth, Md., 1763.

ANDREW HESSELIUS, nephew of Bsp. Svedberg; sett. Wilmington, Del., Old Swedes' Chh., 1713-1723; Chester, Pa., Chh. at Upland, 1713-1723; S.P.G. missionary at Hwitler Kill, Pa., St. James' Chh., 1720-1723; returned to Sweden, 1723; sett. Gagnef, 1723; Sw. Luth.

SAMUEL HESSELIUS, b. Delacarlien, Sweden; nephew of Bsp. Svedberg; Ord. Skara, Sweden, Apr. 27, 1718; arriv. Philadelphia, Dec. 3, 1719; sett. Philadelphia, Pa., Gloria Dei Chh., asst., 1719-1723; Southampton, Pa., Neshaminy Dutch Reformed Chh. at Churchville, 1719-1721; Molatton, Pa., Sw. Luth. Chh., now St. Gabriel's Chh. at Manathanim, Douglassville, 1720-inst. Oct. 1723-1731; New Hanover, Pa., Faulkner's Swamp Luth. Chh., 1720-1723; Wilmington, Del., Old Swedes' Chh., 1723-1731; Chester, Pa., Chh. at Upland, 1723-1731; Chester, Pa., St. Paul's Chh. 1726-1728; returned to Sweden after Oct. 10, 1731; sett. Rumfertuna (Westeras) Sweden, 1731; Sw. Luth.

ISRAEL HOLGH, sett. Wilmington, Del., Old Swedes' Chh., 1644-1646; Tinicum, Pa., Sw. Luth. Chh., 1647-1650; Sw. Luth.

HENRY HOOK, b. Ireland, Ord. Ireland, 1718; sett. Fairfield, N. J., Chh. at Cohansey, 1718-1722; Greenwich, N. J., 1718-1722; New Castle, Del., 1st Chh., 1723-1726; Drawyer's Creek, Del., inst. Sept. 14, 1724-1741; Appoquinimink, Del., 1724-1741; Chester Town, Kent, Md., 1737-1741; Presb.; d. Drawyer's Creek, Del., 1741.

JOHN HUETT (Hewett), son of Rev. John Huett, D.D. (1614-1658) of St. Gregory's by St. Paul's, London; came to Md., ca. 1677; sett. Stepney Parish, Md., 1682-(1st baptism there Jan. 25, 1682/3)-1695; Somerset Parish, Md., Chhs. at Princess Anne and Monie, 1691-1695; Dorchester Parish, Md., 1691-1695; Laurel, Del., Christ Chh. or Broad Creek Chh. at Little Creek, 1685-1695; Ep.; d. Somerset Parish, Md., 1697/8 (inventory, June 29, 1698).

JOHN HUSSEY, Friends' minister at New Castle, Del., 1703, and at Woodbridge, N. J., 1723; visited Nantucket Island, Mass., in 1703 and 1723, as a Quaker preacher; Friend.

ALEXANDER HUSTON (Houston), Ord. Murderkill (Kent)

Del., Oct. 9, 1764-1785; Milford, Del., Chh. at Three Runs, 1764-1785; Presb.; d. Murderkill, Del., Jan. 3, 1785.

BISHOP CHARLES INGLIS, D.D., b. Glenkilcar, Donegal, Ireland, ca. 1734, son of Rev. Archibald Inglis; came to Am., 1755; A.B., (Hon) Columbia, 1767, A.M., Oxford, Apr. 6, 1770, D.D., Oxford, Feb. 25, 1778; schoolmaster in Am., 1756; Ord. London, 1759; K.B. Pa., Jan. 10, 1759; sett. Dover, Del., 1759-1765; Smyrna, Del., St. Peter's Chh., 1759-1764; Mispillion, Del., Christ Chh., 1759-1764; Milford, Del., Christ Chh., 1759-1764; New York, N. Y., Trinity Chh., Dec. 6, 1765-1783; 1st Bsp. of Nova Scotia, Aug. 12, 1787-1816; Ep.; d. Halifax, N. S., Feb. 24, 1816, ae. 82.

ROBERT JAMISON, b. Ireland; Ord. 1734; sett. Duck Creek, Del., Dec. 26, 1734-1744; Dover, Del., 1734-1744; Smyrna, Del., 1734-1744; Presb.; d. Duck Creek, Del., 1744.

DAVID JENISON, sett. Duck Creek, Del., 1745-1748; Presb.

THOMAS JENKINS, b. St. Davids, Wales, ca. 1682; K.B. N. J., Jan. 27, 1706/7; sett. Appoquinimink, Del., 1707-1709; Middletown, Del., St. Anne's Chh., 1707-1709; New Castle, Del., Immanuel Chh., 1708-1709; Ep.; d. Appoquinimink, Del., July 30, 1709.

GRIFFTH JONES, b. Alltfawr, Llanon, Carmarthon, Wales, Oct. 8, 1696; came to Am., 1749; sett. Kenton Hundred, Del., Dutch Creek or Bryn Zion Chh., 1749-1757; Bapt.; d. Duck Creek, Del., Dec. 4, 1757, bur. at Pencader, Del.

JOHN KING, came from London, 1769, itinerant minister in Del., N. J., Va., Md., and N. C., 1772-1800; preached, Eastern Shore, Md., Dec. 24, 1772, Frederick, Md., 1773; sett. Trenton, N. J., Green St. Chh., 1773-1775; Meth.; d. near Raleigh, N. C., ca. 1800.

ROBERT LAING (See C.C.Md.); sett. Brandywine and White Clay, 1722; Presb.

JOSIAH LEWIS, A.B., A.B., Princeton, 1766; sett. Blackwater, Del., 1771-1774; Presb.

REES LEWIS, sett. Duck Creek Chh., Del., 1744-1744; Presb.

JOHN ABRAHAM LIDENIUS, sett. Swedesborough, N. J., Trinity Chh. on Racoon Creek, now Ep., 1713-1724, 1751-1762; Pennsneck, N. J., St. George's Chh., now Ep., 1713-1724; 1755-1762; Wilmington, Del., Old Swedes' Chh., now Ep., 1713-1716; Chester, Pa., Chh., at Upland, 1713-1716; went to Sweden, 1724, but returned by 1751; sett. Molatton, Pa., St. Gabriel's Chh., Douglassville, 1752-1755; Penn, Pa., St. John's Chh., Ep., 1755-1760; Marcus Hook, Pa., 1756-1759; Sw. Luth.

WILLIAM LINDSAY, A.M., Glasgow U., A.B., A.M.; came to Am., 1733; sett. Bristol (Bucks) Pa., June 8, 1735-1745; S.P.G. at Lancaster, Pa., 1734-Feb. 21, 1735; London Grove, Pa., 1735-1745; Penn, Pa., St. John's Chh., 1735-1745; Mill Creek, Del., St. James' Chh. at Stanton, 1735-1745; Alexandria, N. J., St. Thomas' Chh., 1735-1745; Amwell, N. J., St. Andrew's Chh., 1735-1745; Hopewell,

N. J., 1735-1745; Trenton, N. J., St. Michael's Chh., 1735-1745; Ep.

LARS LOCK (Lawrence Karlsson Lockenius), a Finn, educated at the Univ. of Upsala; sett. Wilmington, Del., Old Swedes' Chh., 1647-1688; Tinicum, Pa., New Goeteborg Chh., 1647-1688; Chester, Pa., Upland Chh., 1647-1669; Philadelphia, Pa., Gloria Dei Chh., 1677-1688; Crane Hook, Del., Chh. at Tran Hook, 1677-1688; for many years after 1650, he was the only clergyman in Pa.; preached both in Swedish and Dutch; Sw. Luth.; d. Wilmington, Del., 1688.

RICHARD LOCKE, K.B., Bermuda, July 4, 1743, lic. for Va., May 13, 1749; missionary, S.P.G. in N. J., and Pa., 1745-1747; sett. Lancaster, Pa., St. James' Chh., Oct. 3, 1744-1749; Caernarvon, Pa., Bangor Chh., 1744-1751; Newtown, Pa., St. David's at Radnor, 1753-1753; returned to England, 1754, for a short visit; sett. Lewes, Del., St. Peter's Chh., 1754-1754; Ep., d. Lewes, Del., 1754.

JOHN LYON, A.B. (poss. a son or younger brother of Rev. James Lyon of Derby, Conn.), A.B., Y.C., 1761; Ord. England, 1764; K.B. for N. E., July 11, 1764; lic. for N. E., June 29, 1765; missionary S.P.G.; sett. Taunton, Mass., St. Thomas' Chh., 1764-1769, and of missionary chapels at Bridgewater and Middleborough; sett. Lewes, Indian River, Dagsboro, Cedar Creek Hundred and Broadkill, all in Sussex Co., Del., 1769-1774; St. George's Parish (Accomac) Va., 1774-1786; Tory; imprisoned for five years by court martial for aiding the enemy; Ep.; d. Va., ca. 1796.

SAMUEL MAGAW, D.D., b. Cumberland Pa., 1735; A.B., U. of Pa., 1757, A.M., D.D., 1783; sett. New Castle (New Castle) Del., 1st Chh., Presb. 1763-1764; Ord. (Ep.) London, 1767; K.B. Pa., Feb. 24, 1767; sett. Dover, Del., Christ Chh., S.P.G., 1767-1779; Smyrna, Del., 1767-1779; Milford, Del., 1767-1774; Mispillion, Del., 1767-1774; Philadelphia, Pa., St. Paul's Chh., Jan. 1781-1804; Vice-Provost, U. of Pa., Prof. of Moral Philosophy, 1782-1792; memb. Am. Phil. Soc., 1784; Presb.-Ep.; d. Philadelphia, Pa., Dec. 1, 1812.

ARCHIBALD McCOOK, came from Ireland; lic. by New Castle Presbytery, Sept. 13, 1726; Ord. Dover, Del., June 7, 1727-1729; Murderkill, Del., 1727-1729; first minister in Kent County, Del., Presb.; d. Dover, Del., Sept. 7, 1729.

JOHN McCREARY, A.M., A.B., Princeton, 1764, A.M., 1773; Ord. 1769; sett. Mill Creek, Del., Chh. at White Clay Creek, 1769-1800; Head of Christiana, White Clay Creek Hundred, Del., 1769-1800; Presb.; d. Head of Christiana, Del., 18, 1800.

ALEXANDER McDOWALL, b. Ireland, lic. July 30, 1740; Ord. Oct. 29, 1741, by Donegal Presbytery as evangelist to Va.; missionary to Va., (prob. at Peeked Mountain, Va., 1741); sett. Nottingham, 1743-1744; Elk River, Md., Rock Chh. at Lewisville, 1744-1760; principal of a school at Elk, Pa. and Newark, Del.; sett. Pencader Hundred, Del., 1767-1773; Bethel, Md., Chh. at Upper Node Forest, 1774; Presb.; d. Newark, Del., Jan. 12, 1782, unm.

DANIEL McGILL, see *C.C.Md.*

WILLIAM McKENNAN, b. Delaware, ca. 1719, lic. before May, 1752; supply at North and South Mountain, Timber Grove, North River, Cook's Creek, John Hinson's, Va., 1752-1753; Ord. White Clay, Del., Dec. 1755-1809; Red Clay Creek, Mill Creek Hundred, Del., 1755-1809; Wilmington, Del., 1st Presb. Chh., 1755-1789; Presb.; d. Red Clay Creek, Del., May 5, 1809, ae. 90 yrs.

JAMES MARTIN, came from Ireland; sett. Lewes, Del., 1734-1743; Cool Spring, Del., 1734-1743; Presb.; d. Lewes, Del., May 1743.

JOHN MILLER, A.M., b. Boston, Mass., Dec. 24, 1722, son of John and Margaret (Bass) Miller; A.M. (Hon) U. of Pa., 1763; Ord. Boston, Mass., Apr. 26, 1749; sett. Dover, Del., 1748-1791; Duck Creek, Del., 1748-1791; Smyrna, Del., 1748-1791; Old Side Presb.; d. Dover, Del., July 22, 1791, ae. 69 (GS).

JOSEPH MONTGOMERY, A.M., A.B., Princeton, 1755, A.M., 1758, A.M., U. of Pa., 1760, A.M., Y.C., 1760; school master, 1757-1758; Tutor, U. of Pa., 1759-1760; lic. Philadelphia Presbytery, 1759; Ord. New Castle, Del., 1761-1785; Christiana Bridge, Del., 1761-1785; Georgetown, Del., inst., Apr. 16, 1769-1777; Brigade Chaplain, Am. Rev., from Delaware, 1776-1780; M.C. from Pa., 1780-1784; Presb.; d. 1794.

ENOCH MORGAN, b. Allt-goch, Lanevennog Parish, Cardigan, Wales, 1676, son of Rev. Morgan ap Rhyddarch of Wales; came to Am., Sept. 8, 1701; sett. Pencader Hundred, Del., Welsh Tract Chh., Nov. 7, 1730-1740; Bapt.; d. Welsh Tract, Del., Mar. 25, 1740.

THEOPHILUS MORRIS, A.B., b. Galway, Ireland, 1705, son of Francis Morris; adm. pens. Trinity Coll., Dublin, June 28, 1722, ae. 17 yrs.; inst. West Haven, Conn., Sept. 13, 1740-1742, as miss. S.P.G.; sett. Dover, Del., 1743-1745; Smyrna, Del., 1743-1745; Ep.; ret. to England.

HUGH NEILL, A.M., A.M. (Hon) Columbia, 1767; sett. N. J. as a Presb.; Ord. London, 1749, lic. Mar. 26, 1750, K.B. Pa., May 2, 1750; sett. Dover, Del., 1750-1756; Milford, Del., 1750-1757; Mispillion, Del., 1750-1757; Smyrna, Del., 1750-1757; Oxford, Pa., Trinity Chh., 1758-1765; Whitemarsh, Pa., St. George's Chh., 1758-1766; St. Paul's Parish (Queen Annes), Md., 1765-1781; Presb.-Ep.; d. Oxford, Pa., 1781.

CORNELISZ PIETER PLOCKHOY, came from Zeirik Zee, Holland; res. London, Eng., 1658-1659; arriv. Horekill, Del., July 28, 1663; sett. Lewes, Del., Chh. at Horekill, 1663-1664; Dutch social reformer; Mennonite; d. Germantown, Pa., ca. 1694.

JOHN PUGH (poss. b. 1700, son of John Pugh of Machynlleth, Montgomery, matric. Jesus Coll., Oxf., Mar. 11, 1719/20, ae. 20; or b. 1701, son of Rev. Thomas Pugh of Hatherly, Gloucestershire, matric. Balliol Coll., Oxf., Mar. 8, 1720/1, ae. 19); sett. Appoquinimink, Del., St. Anne's Chh., 1734-1745; Middletown, Del., St. Anne's

Chh. at Appoquinimink Creek, 1734-1745; Ep.; d. Appoquinimink, Del., Aug. 30, 1745.

JOHN CHRISTOPHER PYRLAEUS, b. Pausa, Voigtland, 1713; educated at U. of Leipsic, 1733-1738; arr. at Bethlehem, Pa., Oct. 19, 1740; Ord. Oley (Berks) Pa., Feb. 11, 1742; sett. Bethlehelm, Pa., 1742-1742; Philadelphia, Pa., 1742-1743; commenced the study of the Mohawk language, Jan. 1743, under Conrad Weiser; taught the Indian School at Freehold, N. J., Feb. 4, 1744-Nov. 1751; itinerant preacher at Burlington, Cranbury, Lawrence (Maidenhead), Middletown, Princeton, Swedish Settlements and Trenton, N. J.; at Dover, Duck Creek and Lewes, Del.; and at Durham, Lower Salford, Southampton, and Upper Providence, at Trappe, all in Pa., 1743-1749; returned to England, where he remained, 1751-1770, and to Germany, 1770, where he d.; student and teacher of Indian languages, especially the Mohawk and Mohican dialects; Moravian; d. Herrenhut, Germany, May 28, 1785.

JOHN RANKIN, b. Newark, Del., Mar. 22, 1750; Univ. Del. before 1775 (Newark Academy); lic. at Murderkill, Del., Nov. 29, 1775; Ord. June 3, 1778; sett. Blackwater, Del., 1774-1794; Buckingham, Md., at Berlin on the Eastern Shore, 1775-1798; Presb.; d. Buckingham, Md., Mar. 2, 1798, ae. 48.

THOMAS READ, D.D., b. Nottingham, Chester Co., Pa., Mar. 1746, son of John and Eleanor Read; A.B., U. of Pa., 1766, A.M., 1780; Tutor, U. of Pa., 1766-1768; A.M. (Hon) Princeton, 1772, D.D., Princeton, 1796; sett. Drawyer's Creek, Del., 1768-1798; Appoquinimink, Del., 1768-1798; Wilmington, Del. (1st Presb. Chh.), 1798-1817; Wilmington (2nd Presb. Chh.), 1817-1823; patriot during the Revolution; President, Newark (Del.) Academy; Presb.; d. Wilmington, Del., June 14, 1823.

PHILIP READING, b. 1720, son of Rev. William Reading of St. Alphage Parish, London; ed. Winchester School, matric. Univ. Coll. Oxford, Mar. 27, 1738, ae. 18 yrs.; K.B. Pa., Apr. 17, 1746; sett. Appoquinimink, Del., St. Anne's Church, 1746-1778; Middletown, Del., 1746-1778; Augustine Parish, Md., 1774-1776; Ep.; d. Appoquinimink, Del., Oct. 29, 1778.

ABRAHAM REINCKE (Reinecke), b. Stockholm, Sweden, Apr. 17, 1712, son of Peter and Margaret (Peterson) Reincke; Univ. of Jena, 1735; became a Moravian, 1738; sett. St. Petersburg, Russia, 1740-1741; London and Yorkshire, England, 1741-1744; arriv. N. Y. C., Oct. 25, 1744; arriv. Bethlehem, Pa., Nov. 9, 1744; Ord. priest, Feb. 1745; sett. Nazareth, Pa., Nov. 1745-June 25, 1747; Philadelphia, Pa., June 1747-Feb. 1749, 1751-1753; Lancaster, Pa., Feb. 1749-Nov. 1750; Lititz, Warwick, Pa., 1749-1753; Wallpack, N. J., 1753-1755; Paulin's Kill, N. J., 1753-1755; Salisbury, N. Y., 1753-1755; Oblong, Amenia Union, N. Y., 1753-1755; Nine Partners, Round Top at Bethel, N. Y., 1753-1755; Livingston Manor, N. Y., 1753-1755; New York, N. Y., 1754-1755; Dansbury, Bethlehem, Pa., 1753-1755; also as an itinerant preacher as follows: 1745-1749, Bethlehem, Durham, Lower Salford, Manatawny, Southampton, and Upper Providence, all in Pa.; Dover, Duck Creek and Lewes, Del.; and Burlington, Cranbury, Great Egg Harbor, Lawrence, Middletown, Princeton, Swedish Settlements and Trenton, N. J.; 1745-1755, Ammasland, Lynn, Swedish Settlements, Pa.; and Bridgeton at Cohansey, Calkoen's Hook, Cape May, Little Egg Harbor, Mauris River, Pennsneck, Swedesboro and Swedish Settlements, N. J.; Moravian; d. Bethlehem, Pa., Apr. 7, 1760.

MATTHEW REUTZ, b. Denmark; arriv. N. Y. C., Nov. 26, 1743; sett. Bethlehem, Pa., 1743-1748; Ord. 1748; sett. Graceham, Md., 1751-1751; Old Man's Creek, N. J., 1751-1753; also an itinerant preacher at the following places: 1743-1747, Philadelphia, Pa.; 1743-1748, Burlington, N. J.; 1743-1749, Cranbury, Lawrence, Middletown, Princeton, in New Jersey, Dover, Duck Creek and Lewes, Delaware, and Durham, Lower Salford, Manatawny, Southampton, Upper Providence, and Swedish Settlements, Pennsylvania; 1745-1749, Cape May, N. J.; 1745-1753, Cohansey, Calkoen's Hook, Little Egg Harbor, Mauris River, Pennsneck, Swedesborough and Swedish Settlements, N. J., and Ammasland, Pa.; 1743-1753, Great Egg Harbor, N. J.; and 1747-1749, Trenton, N. J.; Moravian; d. Old Man's Creek, N. J., Oct. 7, 1753.

OWEN RICE, came from Haverfordwest, Wales, to Bethlehem, Pa., 1742; Ord. (deacon) 1748; sett. Southampton, Pa., 1742-1744; Philadelphia, Pa., 1749-1751; Staten Island, N. Y., 1751-1752; New York, N. Y., 1751-1754; itinerant preacher in English at New York City, 1742-1748, and generally during these years at the following places: Ammasland, Durham, Lower Salford, Manatawny, Upper Providence and Swedish Settlements, all in Pa.; at Dover, Duck Creek and Lewes, Del.; and the following places in New Jersey: Cohansey, Burlington, Calkoen's Hook, Cape May, Great Egg Harbor, Lawrence, Little Egg Harbor, Mauris River, Middletown, Pennsneck, Princeton, Swedesborough, Swedish Settlements and Trenton; he returned to Europe, 1754, and served congregations in England and Ireland, 1754-1785; physician, surgeon; Moravian; d. Gomersal, Yorkshire, England, 1785.

WILLIAM ROBINSON, b. near Carlisle, England, ca. 1700, son of a Quaker physician; educated at the Log College; school master at Hopewell, N. J., 1728-1739; lic. Neshaminy, May 27, 1740; Ord. New Brunswick, N. J., Aug. 4, 1741; itinerant missionary in Va. and the Carolinas; first known Presb. minister to preach in N. C.; sett. Cub Creek (Charlotte) Va., Chh. at Round Oak, 1742-1743; St. George's, Del., 1743-1746, this church having split off from Drawyer's Creek Church; New Side Presb.; d. St. George's, Del., Aug. 1, 1746.

JOHN RODGERS, D.D., b. Boston, Mass., Aug. 5, 1727, son of Thomas and Elizabeth (Baxter) Rodgers; grad. Academy at Fagg's Manor, 1743; A.M., Princeton, 1760, A.M., U. of Pa., 1763; D.D., U. of Edinburgh, 1768; lic. New Castle Presbytery, Oct. 14, 1747;

Ord. St. George's, Del., Mar. 16, 1748/9-May 18, 1765; sett. Appoquinimink, Del., 1748-1765; Middletown, Del., Forest Church, 1749-1765; Taylor's Bridge, Del., 1750-1765; inst. New York, N. Y., 1st Presb. Chh., Sept. 4, 1765-1811; N. Y. C., 2nd Presb. Chh., 1767-1810; Trustee, Princeton U., 1765-1807; Chaplain of a N. Y. Regt., 1776-1777; Vice-Chancellor, Univ. State of N. Y., 1787-1811; Moderator of the Presb. General Assembly, 1789; Presb.; d. N. Y. C., May 7, 1811, ae. 83.

JOHN REINHOLD RONNER, Ord. (Deacon), Bethlehem, Pa., 1743; sett. Dansbury, Pa., 1748-1749 and Wallpack, N. J., 1748-1749 (including Tulpehocken, Muddy Creek, the Minnisinks, and Warwick, 1743-1750); St. Thomas, West Indies, 1755-1756; Bethlehem, Pa., 1755-1756; also was an itinerant preacher in the following places, 1743-1748: Duck Creek, Dover and Lewes, Del.; Burlington, Cranbury, Lawrence, Middletown, Princeton, Swedish Settlements and Trenton, N. J.; and Durham, Lower Salford, Manatawny, Philadelphia, Southampton and Upper Providence, Pa.; Moravian; d. Bethlehem, Pa., July, 1756.

AENEAS ROSS, son of the Rev. George Ross (q.v.); Ord. London, 1739; K.B. Pa., Feb. 26, 1740/1; sett. Bristol, Pa., St. James the Greater Chh., 1740-1741; Philadelphia, Pa. (Christ Chh.), June 1741-June 1743; Oxford, Pa., Trinity Chh., 1742-1758; Whitemarsh, Pa., St. Thomas' Chh., 1742-1758; New Castle, Del., 1757-1782; Ep.; d. New Castle, Del., ca. 1782.

GEORGE ROSS, A.M., b. Balblair, Scotland, 1679, son of David Ross; A.B., Edinburgh, 1700, A.M.; Ord. London, 1700; Chaplain, Royal Navy; K.B. N. J., May 2, 1705; arriv. Philadelphia, Aug. 23, 1705; sett. New Castle, Del., 1705-1708; 1713-1753; Chester, Pa., St. Paul's Chh., 1708-1714; Concord, Pa., St. John's Chh., 1708-1712; North Elk Parish, Md., 1731-1733; prisoner in France, 1711; Missionary, V.S.P.G.F.P.; Ep.; d. New Castle, Del., 1753, ae. 72.

JOHN SCOTT, son of Rev. James Scott, of Virginia; K.B. Md., Apr. 1, 1769; sett. Laurel, Del., Christ Chh., Nov. 22, 1770-1775; Tory in the Rev.; sett. Dettingen Parish (Prince William) Va., 1782-1783; Ep., d. Dettingen Par., Va., soon after 1783.

RICHARD SEWALL, induct. North Sassafras Parish, Md., St. Stephen's Chh., June 1, 1697-1723; Appoquinimink, Del., 1704-1707; Middletown, Del., 1704-1707; Shrewsbury Parish (Kent) Md., induct. May 20, 1709-1713, Sept. 3, 1723-1724; Wye Mills (Talbot) Md., St. Luke's Chh., 1723-1724; Ep.

ELIZABETH SHIPLEY, Friends' minister at Wilmington, Del., 1760; visited Nantucket Island, Mass., 1760, as a Quaker preacher; Friend.

ROBERT SINCLARE (St. Clare), b. ca. 1685; tutor to Lord Crichton; K.B. Pa., Aug. 31, 1709; missionary, V.S.P.G.F.P.; sett. New Castle, Del., 1710-1712; resigned; Ep.

MATTHEW SITTENSPERGER, alias Manners, b. Germany;

sett. Lancaster, Pa., St. John Nepomucene's Chh., 1748-1752; Conowago, Pa., Sacred Heart Chh., 1753-1758; Mill Creek, Del., St. Mary's Chapel, at Coffee Run, Jan. 1772-1786; Mill Creek, Del., St. John's Chh. at Mt. Cuba or Cuba Rock, Jan. 1772-1786; R.C.

JOSEPH SMITH, A.B., b. Nottingham, Pa., 1736; A.B., Princeton, 1764; lic. Aug. 5, 1767; Ord. Lower Brandywine, Del., Apr. 19, 1769-Aug. 22, 1772; Brandywine, 1769-Apr. 1778; Wilmington, Del., 2nd Presb. Chh. (fdr. 1773), Oct. 27, 1774-Apr. 29, 1778; sett. Buffalo and Cross Creek, Pa., June 21, 1779-1792; fdr. Jefferson Coll., 1791; Presb.; d. Buffalo, Washington Co., Pa., Apr. 19, 1792.

THOMAS SMITH, A.M., A.B., Princeton, 1758, A.M.; inst. Cranbury, N. J., 1762-1789; Pennsneck, N. J., 1762-1789; St. George's, Del., 1769-1774; Presb.; d. Cranbury, N. J., Dec. 23, 1789.

ELIHU SPENCER, D.D., b. Millington Parish, East Haddam, Conn., Feb. 21, 1721/2, son of Dea. Isaac and Mary (Selden) Spencer; A.B., Y.C., 1746, A.M., D.D., U. of Pa., 1782; Trustee of Princeton, 1752-1784; Ord. Boston, Mass., Sept. 14, 1748, as a missionary to the Oneidas; inst. Elizabethtown, N. J., 1st Chh., Cong.-Presb., Feb. 7, 1749/50-1756; Jamaica, L. I., N. Y., 1756-1758; Shrewsbury, N. J., Nov. 1759-1764; Middletown, N. J., at Middletown Point, 1759-1764; Shark River, N. J., 1759-1764; Perth Amboy, N. J., 1759-1764; St. George's, Del., 1764-inst. Apr. 17, 1766-1769; Middletown, Del., Forest Chh., 1764-Oct. 19, 1769; Appoquinimink, Del., 1764-1767; inst. Trenton, N. J., 1st Presb. Chh., Nov. 18, 1769-1784; Hopewell, Ewing, 1769-1784; Lawrenceville, N. J., Maidenhead Chh., 1769-1784; Chaplain, 1758, 1777; Presb., d. Trenton, N. J., Dec. 27, 1784, ae. 63 (GS).

HUGH STEVENSON, came from Ireland to Am., 1726; lic. Sept. 13, 1726; New Castle, Del., 1727-1728; also at Lewes, Del., Nottingham, Pa.; Ord. Snow Hill, Md., before June 1729; sett. Snow Hill, 1728-1733; Potomac Chh., Northumberland Co., Va., 1733; teacher at Philadelphia, 1739-1744; Presb.; d. Philadelphia, Pa., May, 1744.

JOHN SUTTON, b. Basking Ridge, N. J., Feb. 12, 1733; educated at Hopewell, N. J.; Ord. Scotch Plains, N. J., 1763; sett. Salem, N. J., 1761-1766; Cape May, N. J., Apr. 1, 1764-1766; Pencader Hundred, Del., Welsh Tract Chh., Nov. 3, 1770-1777; Kenton Hundred, Del., 1770-1777; Simpson's Creek, Va., 1777-1788; went to Kentucky, 1788; see *Hist. . . . Baptists of Kentucky*, II 42; Bapt., d. Kentucky, ca. 1800.

CHARLES TENNENT, b. Colrain, Co. Down, Ireland, May 3, 1711, son of Rev. William and Catharine (Kennedy) Tennent; educated at the Log Coll., by his father; lic. Sept. 20, 1736; Ord. White Clay, Del., soon after Apr. 6, 1737; sett. Mill Creek, Del., White Clay Creek, 1736-1762; Christiana Bridge, Del., 1736-1756; Blackwater, Del., 1763-1767; Buckingham, Md., at Berlin, Eastern Shore, 1763-1767; Laurel, Del., 1767-Nov. 1769 and Little Creek, Del.; Presb.; d. Buckingham, Md., Feb. 25, 1771, ae. 59.

THE COLONIAL CLERGY OF DELAWARE 85

GILBERT TENNENT, D.D., b. Co. Armagh, Ireland, Feb. 5, 1702/3, son of Rev. William and Catharine (Kennedy) Tennent; came to Am. ae. 14 yrs.; A.M. (Hon) Y.C., 1725; D.D.; lic. Philadelphia, May 1725; Ord. New Brunswick, N. J., 1726-1743; New Castle, Del., 1726-1727; Philadelphia, Pa., 2nd Presb. Chh., Whitefield Society, May 1743-1764; went on a preaching tour to Boston, 1740; went abroad to solicit funds for Princeton, 1753; trustee, Princeton U., 1746-1764; Old Side Presb.; d. Philadelphia, Feb. 10, 1764, ae. 62 (GS).

PETER TESSCHENMAEKER, educated at the Universities of Leyden, 1669, Groeningen, 1671, Utrecht, 1671-1673; Ord. South River, N. J., Oct. 9, 1679 (first Dutch Reformed minister ordained in America); sett. Kingston, N. Y., Esopus Chh., 1675-1676, Apr.-Sept. 1678; Guiana, S.A., 1676-1678; New Castle, Del., 1st Chh., 1679-1682; Staten Island, N. Y., D. R. Chh. at Port Richmond, 1680-1682; Staten Island, F.R. Chh. at Fresh Kills, 1682-1683; Staten Island, F.R. Chh. at South Side, 1682-1683; Schenectady, N. Y., 1682-1690/1; Hackensack, N. J., Chh. at New Barbardoes, 1686-1687; D.R.; massacred by the Indians at Schenectady, N. Y., Feb. 8, 1690/1.

DANIEL THANE, A.M., b. Scotland; educated at Aberdeen; A.B., Princeton, 1748, A.M.; Ord. Connecticut Farms, N. J., Aug. 29, 1750-1756; instl. New Castle, Del., May 1, 1757-1763; White Clay Creek, Del., New Side Chh., 1757-1763; Christiana Bridge, Del., 1757-1763; New Side Presb.; d. Delaware, 1764.

ELISHA THOMAS, b. Caermarthen, Wales, 1674; arriv. in Am., Sept. 8, 1701; sett. Pencader Hundred, Del., Welsh Tract Chh., July 25, 1725-1730; Bapt.; d. Welsh Tract, Del., Nov. 7, 1730.

OWEN THOMAS, b. Gwrgodllys, Cilmanllwyd, Pembroke, Wales, 1692; came to Am., 1707; sett. Pencader Hundred, Del., Welsh Tract Chh., 1740-May 27, 1748; Newlin, Pa., Hephzibah Chh., 1748-1759; Yellow Springs, Maryland, 1748-1760; Vincent, Pa., 1748-1760; Bapt.; d. Vincent, Pa., Nov. 12, 1760, a. 68 (GS).

JOHN THOMSON, b. Sept. 1690, came from Co. Down, Ireland to N. Y., 1715; Ord. Lewes, Del., Apr. 1717-1729; Bart, Pa., Middle Octorara Chh., 1730-1732; Chestnut Level, Pa., Drumore Chh., 1732-July 31, 1744; North Middleton, Pa., Meeting House Springs Chh., 1735-1735; Opequon Creek, Va., near Winchester, 1739-1739; Cub Creek, Va., Round Oak Chh., 1744-1753; Buffalo, Va., 1744-1753; Concord, Va., 1744-1753; made missionary visits to N. C., 1744, 1751, 1753; Moderator of the Presb. Chh. of America, 1722; d. Centre, N. C., 1753.

SYDENHAM THORN, K.B. Pa., Sept. 12, 1774; sett. Philadelphia, Pa., St. Paul's Chh., 1774-1781; Milford, Del., Christ Chh., 1774-1781; Mispillion, Del., 1774-1781; Ep.

SAMUEL TINGLEY, b. New York, ca. 1745; Ord. 1773; K.B. N. J., Mar. 12, 1773; sett. Lewes, Broadkill, Cedar Creek, Dagsboro, and Indian River, Del., 1774-1783; Somerset Parish, Md., 1783-1785; Coventry Parish, Md., 1785-1796; Stepney Parish, Md., 1796-1798; Worcester Parish, Md., 1798-1800; Ep.; d. Worcester Parish, Md., 1800, a. ca. 55 yrs.

REORUS TORKILLUS, b. Faessberg, Sweden, 1609; studied at Lidkoeping; sett. Skara, Sweden; chaplain at Goeteborg, Sweden; came to Am., 1638/9; sett. Wilmington, Del., 1st minister of Old Swedes' Chh., Mar. 1638/9-1643; first Lutheran minister in North America; Sw. Luth.; d. Fort Christiana, Del., Sept. 7, 1643.

PETER TRANBERG, sett. Swedesboro, N. J., Trinity Chh. on Raccoon Creek, 1726-1741; Pennsneck, N. J., St. George's Chh., 1726-1741; Wilmington, Del., Old Swedes Chh., 1742-1748; Chester, Pa., Upland Chh., 1742-1748; preached in German, Swedish and English; Sw. Luth.; d. Pennsneck, N. J., Nov. 8, 1748.

GEORGE TROTTER, K.B. Md., Jan. 11, 1697/8; sett. Laurel, Del., Christ Chh., Broad Creek and Little Creek, 1696-1703; Somerset Parish, Md., Chhs. at Princess Anne and Monie, 1696-1703; Stepney Parish, Md., 1696-1703; All Faiths' Parish (St. Mary's) Md., 1703-1707; Ep.

MOSES TUTTLE, A.M., b. New Haven, Conn., June 25, 1715; A.B., Y.C., 1745, A.M.; see *C.C.N.E.*, p. 210; sett. Laurel, Del., Presb. Chh., 1756-Sept. 1762; preached in N. J., May 1764-May 1769; Cong.-Presb.; d. Southold, L. I., N. Y., Nov. 21, 1785, ae. 70.

ERIC UNANDER, sett. Swedesboro, N. J., 1749-1755; Pennsneck, N. J., 1749-1756; Marcus Hook, Pa., 1749-1756; Chester, Pa., Upland Chh., 1755-1759; Wilmington, Del., Old Swedes' Chh., 1755-1760; left for Sweden, July, 1760; Sw. Luth.

ARTHUR USSHER, A.M., b. Co. Waterford, Ireland, 1705, son of James Ussher, Gent.; pens. Trinity Coll., Dublin, June 9, 1724, ae. 19 yrs.; scholar, 1727, A.B., 1728, A.M., 1734; K.B. Feb. 10, 1736/7; sett. Dover, Del., 1737-1743; Milford, Del., 1740-1743; Mispillion, Del., 1740-1743; Smyrna, Del., 1740-1743; Lewes, Del., 1744-1752; Broadkill, Del., 1744-1752; Cedar Creek, Del., 1744-1752; Dagsboro, Del., 1744-1752; Indian River, Del., 1744-1752; Newton, Pa., St. David's Chh. at Radnor, 1749-1753; resigned, 1753; Ep.

RICHARD UTLEY, b. Yorkshire, England, Feb. 22, 1720; became a Moravian, 1742; arriv. Staten Island, N. Y., Nov. 26, 1743; Ord. Deacon, Philadelphia, Pa., Aug. 14, 1746; sett. New York, N. Y., 1743-1748; Lancaster, Pa., 1748-1748; Oley, Pa., 1749-1750; Philadelphia, Pa., 1749-1752, 1762-1774; Graceham, Md., 1752-1755, 1770-1771; Staten Island, 1755-1755; Newport, R. I., 1758-1758; Bethabara, N. C., 1766-1770; Salem, N. C., 1772-1775; also an itinerant preacher at the following places between the years 1743-1749: Dover, Duck Creek and Lewes, Del.; Burlington, Cranbury, Lawrence, Middletown, Princeton, Swedish Settlements and Trenton, N. J.; and Durham, Lower Salford, Manatawny, Southampton and Upper Providence, Pa.; Moravian; d. Salem, N. C., Oct. 9, 1775.

RUDOLPHUS VARICK, matric. U. of Utrecht, 1666; in East Indies, 1673-1678; at Hem, Holland, 1679-1686; arriv. North America, July, 1686; sett. at the following places on Long Island, N. Y., 1686-1694: Brooklyn, Bushwick, Flatbush, Flatlands, Gravesend and New Utrecht; also on Staten Island, N. Y., at Port Richmond, 1686-1694; New Castle, Del., 1687-1687; and Hackensack, N. J., 1687-1689; Dutch Reformed; d. Long Island, N. Y., Aug. 1694.

EVERARDUS WELIUS, matric. U. Leyden, 1647; Ord. Amsterdam, Holland, Apr. 10, 1647; called as minister to New Castle (then called New Amstel), Del., Apr. 10, 1657; arriv. Am., 1657; sett. New Castle, Del., 1657-1659; Dutch Reformed; d. New Castle, Del., Dec. 9, 1659.

JAMES WILSON, son of Matthew Wilson of Philadelphia, Pa.; sett. Blackwater, Del., 1768-1771; New London, Pa., inst. Oct. 15, 1771-Oct. 27, 1778; New Londonderry, Pa., 1771-1778; Presb.

JOHN WILSON, b. Scotland; sett. New Castle, Del., 1st Chh., 1700-1710; Appoquinimink, Del., 1708-1712; Drawyer's Creek, Del., 1708-1712; Head of Christiana, Del., 1708-1712; White Clay Creek, Del., 1708-1712; New Side Presb.; d. White Clay, Del., 1712, s.p.

MATTHEW WILSON, D.D., b. East Nottingham, Pa., Jan. 15, 1731, son of James and Jean Wilson; educated at New London, Pa., A.M., U. of Pa., 1760, D.D., U. of Pa., 1786; Ord. Delaware, before May 1755; inst. Lewes, Del., Apr. 1756-1790; Cool Spring, Del., 1756-1790; Indian River, Del., Aug. 1767-1790; physician, teacher and lawyer; Old Side Presb.; d. Lewes, Del., Mar. 30, 1790, ae. 59 yrs.

ROBERT WITHERSPOON, b. Scotland; Ord. Drawyer's Creek, St. George's Hundred, Del., May 13, 1714-1718; sett. Appoquinimink, Del., 1714-1718; Presb.; d. Drawyer's Creek, Del., May 1718.

THOMAS YARREL (Yarrell), an Englishman, arriv. Bethlehem, Pa., 1742; Ord. Deacon, 1755; sett. Mt. Joy, Pa., Donegal Chh., 1745-1746; Philadelphia, Pa., 1754-1756; New York, N. Y., 1757-1765; Staten Island, N. Y., 1757-1760, 1762-1763; Newport, R. I., 1758-1763; also as itinerant minister at the following places, 1743-1755: Dover, Duck Creek and Lewes, Del.; Bridgeton, Burlington, Calkoen's Hook, Cape May, Cranbury, Great Egg Harbor, Lawrence, Little Egg Harbor, Mauris River, Middletown, Pennsneck, Princeton, Swedesboro, Swedish Settlements and Trenton, all in N. J.; and Ammasland, Lower Salford, Manatawny, Southampton, Swedish Settlements and Upper Providence, Pa.; returned to England, 1766, and was settled in England and Scotland; preached in English; Moravian.

JOHN YEO, A.B., son of a minister, matric. Exeter Coll., Oxford, Mar. 29, 1656; A.B., 1659; Rector, Wear Gifford, Devon, 1661; arriv. Md., 1675; sett. Christ Chh. Par. (Calvert) Md., 1675-1678; All Faiths' Par. (St. Mary's) Md., 1675-1678; New Castle, Del.,

June 4, 1678-1683; St. John's Par. (Baltimore) Md., Copley Parish, 1683-1686; St. George's Par. (Harford) Md., at Spesutia, 1683-1686; first Episcopal minister in Delaware, settled June 4, 1678; d. St. John's Par. (Balt.) Md., 1686.

SAMUEL YOUNG, came from the Armagh Presbytery in Ireland, Sept. 23, 1718; sett. Drawyer's Creek, St. George's Hundred, Del., 1719-1721; Appoquinimink, Del., 1719-1721; Elk River, Del., 1721-1721; Presb.; d. Drawyer's Creek, Del., before June 6, 1721.

THE COLONIAL CLERGY OF GEORGIA, 1733-1776

JOHN ALEXANDER, K.B. Ga., May 1, 1766; sett. St. John's Parish, Ga., 1766-1766; Ep.

JOHN ALISON, b. 1730; inst. Wilton, S. C., May 1, 1759-1761; sett. Altamaha, Ga., 1761-1766; James Island, S. C., 1766-1766; Presb.; d. James Island, S. C., Oct. 17, 1766, a. 36.

BISHOP JOHN PETER BOEHLER (See *C.C.Del.*), arriv. at Savannah, Ga., Oct. 15, 1738; sett. Savannah, Oct. 1738-Jan. 1739; Moravian; d. London, England, Apr. 27, 1775.

JOHN MARTIN BOLZIUS (Boltzius), b. Dec. 15, 1703; teacher at Halle; Ord. Wernigerode, Nov. 11, 1733; deputy-Superintendent of the Orphan House at Halle; installed over the congregation which came to Georgia, at Rotterdam, Nov. 27, 1733; left Dover, Eng., for Am., Dec. 28, 1733; arriv. Charleston, S. C., Mar. 1, 1733/4; sett. Ebenezer, Ga., 1734-1764; Luth.; d. Ebenezer, Ga., Nov. 19, 1765.

THOMAS BOSOMWORTH, licensed to perform "all religious and ecclesiastical offices in Georgia" by the Bishop of London, July 4, 1743; K.B. Ga., July 6, 1743; sett. Frederica, Ga., 1743-1744; S.P.G. missionary; resigned and returned to England, 1744; Ep.

EDMUND BOTSFORD, A.M., b. Wooburn, Bedforshire, Eng., Nov. 1745; A.M., Brown U., 1802; lic. Feb. 24, 1771; arriv. Charleston, S. C., Jan. 1766; Ord. Charleston, S. C., Mar. 14, 1773; sett. Tuckaseeking, Ga., 1771-1773; New Savannah, Ga., 1773-1777; Brier Creek, Ga., 1777-1779; sett. Welsh Neck Chh., Society Hill, S. C., 1782-1797; Georgetown, S. C., 1797-1819; serv. in Continental army; Bapt.; d. Georgetown, S. C., Dec. 25, 1819, a. 74.

MR. CLAYTON, sett. Tuckaseeking, Ga., 1759-1764; Edisto, S. C., 1764; 7th Day Bapt.

JONATHAN COPP, A.B., bapt. Montville, Conn., Aug. 1, 1725, son of Jonathan and Margaret Copp; A.B., Yale, 1744; Ord. (Bsp. of London), Dec. 27, 1750; K.B. Ga., Feb. 12, 1750/1; S.P.G. missionary; sett. Augusta, Ga., 1750-1755; St. John's Parish (Colleton) S. C., Jan. 28, 1756-1762; preacher at 9th ann. meeting of Clergy of S. C., 1757; Ep.; d. St. John's Parish (Colleton) S. C., Jan. 4, 1762, a. 36.

JOHN ULRICH DRIESLER, sett. St. Simon's Island, Ga., at Frederica, 1744-1746; schoolmaster at Frederica, 1744-1746; Luth.; d. Frederica, St. Simon's Island, Ga., 1746.

WILLIAM DUNCANSON, A.B., b. Co. Cork, Ireland, 1714, son of Rev. Peter Duncanson; pens. Trinity Coll., Dublin, July 12, 1733, a. 19; A.B., 1738; sett. Savannah, Ga., 1761-1761, and Augusta, Ga., 1761-1761, as S.P.G. miss.; Ep.; went to S. C.

JAMES EDMONDS (Edmunds), b. London, Eng., ca. 1720; sett. Wando River, S. C., Dec. 9, 1753-1754; Ord. Charleston, S. C., Independant, Congregational-Presbyterian, Church, Feb. 1755; sett. Charleston, 1754-1767; Altahama, Ga., Aug. 9, 1767-1770; Sunbury, Ga., 1767-1770; Midway, Ga., 1767-1770; itinerant missionary and supply, Presb. Chhs., S. C.; d. Charleston, S. C., Apr. 1793, ae. 73.

EDWARD ELLINGTON, K.B. Ga., May 12, 1767; S.P.G. miss.; sett. Augusta, Ga., 1767-1770; St. Bartholomew's Parish (Colleton) S. C., Dec. 15, 1770-Apr. 1772; St. Helena's Parish (Beaufort) S. C., Apr. 20, 1772-Oct. 22, 1772; St. James's Parish (Berkeley) S. C., at Goose Creek, Apr. 16, 1775-1793; remov. to Savannah, Ga., 1793; Ep.; d. Savannah, Ga.

SAMUEL FRINK, A.M., b. Rutland District, Mass., Nov. 11, 1735, son of Rev. Thomas and Isabell (Wright) Frink; A.B., H. C., 1758, A.M.; became an Episcopalian; sett. Augusta, Ga., 1765-1766; Savannah, Ga., 1767-1771; S.P.G. miss.; d. Savannah, Ga., Oct.-Nov., 1771.

RICHARD GREGORY, son of John Gregory, of Broad River, S. C.; sett. Tuckaseeking, Ga., 1758-1764; Edisto, S. C., 1764; 7th Day. Bapt.

ISRAEL CHRISTIAN GRONAU, tutor, Orphan House at Halle; arriv. Ga., Mar. 1, 1733/1734; sett. Ebenezer, Ga., 1734-1745; Luth.; d. Ebenezer, Ga., Jan. 11, 1745.

HENRY HERBERT, D.D., arriv. Savannah, Ga., with the first colonists, Jan. 1732/3; sett. Savannah, Ga., Mar. 1733-Oct. 1733, at Yamacraw Bluff on the Savannah River, Feb. 12, 1733; Ep.; d. on the return trip to England.

JOHN HOLMES (b. 1745, son of Rev. John Holmes of Haslingden, Lancashire, matric. Brasenose Coll., Oxford, Mar. 7, 1763, a. 18; A.B., 1766, A.M., 1769, Fellow, B.D. and D.D., 1786); K.B. Ga., Aug. 17, 1773; sett. St. George's Parish, Ga., 1773-1777; Ep. (returned to Eng.; rector, St. Mary Whitechapel, London; d. London, Aug. 17, 1795).

WILLIAM HUTSON, b. Eng., Aug. 14, 1720, son of a minister; studied law; sett. Orphan House, Ga., 1743-1743; Ord. Prince William's Parish, S. C., Stoney Creek Chh., May 20, 1743-1757; Charleston, S. C., Independent Chh., 1757-1761; Presb.; d. Charleston, S. C., Apr. 11, 1761, a. 41 (GS).

JOHN McLEOD, came from Isle of Skye, Scotland; Chaplain of a Highland Regt.; Ord. Edinburgh, Scotland, Oct. 13, 1735; sett. Darien, Ga., 1735-1741; Edisto Island, S. C., 1741-1767; Presb.

HERMANN HENRY LEMBKE, student at Halle and teacher

there; came to Am., 1746; sett. Ebenezer, Ga., 1746-1775; Luth.; d. Ebenezer, Ga., ca. 1775.

ABRAHAM MARSHALL, b. Windsor, Conn., Apr. 23, 1748, son of the Rev. Daniel Marshall; lic. 1774; Ord. Kioka (now Kiokee), Ga., 1775, as an evangelist; sett. Kioka, Ga., 1775-1819; Rev. soldier; Trustee, U. Ga.; Bapt.; d. Kiokee, Ga., 1819.

DANIEL MARSHALL, b. Windsor, Conn., 1706; Deacon in the Cong. Chh. at Windsor, Conn., 20 yrs. and miss. to the Indians at Onnaquaggy, N. Y., 1753-1754; Ord. Abbot's Creek, N. C., 1757-1760; Beaver Creek, S. C., 1760-1771; Horse Creek, S. C. (ca. 15 m. n. of Augusta, Ga.), 1760-1771; supply, Shallow Fords (Yadkin) N. C., ca. 1772; sett. Kiokee Creek, Ga., Jan. 1, 1771-1784; Bapt.; d. Kiokee, Ga., Nov. 2, 1784, a. 78.

JOHN NICHOLAS MARTIN, b. Zweibrucken, Lorraine, France; Ord. by the Salzburgers at Ebenezer, Ga.; sett. Waxhaw (Union) N. C., 1750-1763; Amelia, S. C., 1750-1763; Fork of Saluda and Broad Rivers, S. C., Zion's Chh. and St. Michael's Chh., 1750-1760, 1767-1774; Savannah, Ga., 1759-1760; Charleston, S. C., St. John's Chh., Nov. 24, 1763-1767, 1774-1778, 1786-1787; Luth.; d. Charleston, S. C., July 27, 1795.

WILLIAM NORRIS (poss. b. 1718, son of John Norris of Nonsuch, Wilts., matric. Merton Coll., Oxf., Mar. 12, 1735/6, a. 16; *or* poss. b. Kilkenny, Ireland, 1712, son of Robert Norris, gent., pens. Trinity Coll., Dublin, June 5, 1731, a. 19, A.B., 1735), K.B. Ga., Aug. 20, 1738; S.P.G.; sett. Savannah, Ga., June 28, 1739-Nov. 1739; Frederica, Ga., Nov. 1739-Jan. 10, 1739/40; Ep.; left Ga., 1741.

CHRISTOPHER ORTON, K.G. Ga., Oct. 2, 1741; sett. Savannah, Ga., July 25, 1742-Aug. 1742; Ep.; d. Savannah, Ga., Aug. 1742.

SAMUEL QUINCY, A.M., Ord. by Bsp. of Carlisle, Oct. 28, 1730; 1st S.P.G. missionary to Ga.; K.B. Ga., Apr. 2, 1733; sett. Savannah, Ga., May 1733-Oct. 1735; St. John's Parish (Colleton) S. C., July 5, 1742-1745; St. George's (Dorchester) S. C., 1746-1747; Charleston, S. C., St. Philip's Chh., July 6, 1747-1749, asst.; preacher 15th visitation, 1745; Ep.

CHRISTIAN RABENHORST, Ord. St. Anna's Chh., Augsburg, Germany, July 28, 1752; arriv. Ebenezer, Ga., 1752; sett. Ebenezer, Ga., 1752-1777; Luth.; d. Ebenezer, Ga., ca. 1777.

ANTON SEIFFERT, b. Thrulichen, Bohemia; went to Herrenhut, thence to Ga.; arriv. Savannah, Ga., Mar. 22, 1734/5; Ord. Savannah, Ga., Feb. 28, 1735/6; sett. Savannah, Ga., 1736-1739; at Bethlehem, Pa., June 25, 1742-1745; returned to Europe, Apr. 8, 1745; served Chhs. in England, Ireland and Holland; first person ordained by a Christian Bishop *in America;* Moravian; d. Zeist, Holland, June 19, 1785.

JAMES SEYMOUR, K.B. S. C., Sept. 25, 1771; S.P.G.; sett. Augusta, Ga., 1771-1779; imprisoned as a Tory, 1779; refugee at

Savannah, 1780-1782, and in Fla., 1783; Ep.; d. on way to the Bahamas, 1784.

HADDON SMITH, K.B. S. C., Sept. 11, 1772; sett. Prince William Town, S. C., 1773; sett. Savannah, Ga., 1772-1775; Tory; Ep.

BENJAMIN STIRK, b. Leeds, Yorkshire, Eng.; sett. Orphan House, Ga., 1760-1767; Goshen (Lincoln) Ga. (18 m. from Savannah), 1767-1770; Bapt.; d. Goshen, Ga., 1770.

CHRISTOPHER FREDERICK TRIEBNER, b. Germany; sett. Ebenezer, Ga., 1769-1779; Tory; went to Eng.; Luth.; d. after 1784.

HENRY BURCHER GABRIEL WARTMANN, arriv. Am., 1753; sett. Lancaster, Pa., Trinity Chh., 1753-Mar. 1753; Reading, Pa., 1753-1753; Muhlenberg, Pa., 1753-1753; Savannah, Ga. (1753)-1760 or later; Charleston, S. C., 1761-1763; Luth.

CHARLES WESLEY, A.M., b. Epworth, Lincolnshire, Eng., 1708, son of Rev. Samuel and Susannah (Annersley) Wesley; matric. Christ Coll., Oxford, June 13, 1726, a. 18 yrs.; A.B., 1730, A.M., Mar. 12, 1732/3; appointed Secretary of Indian affairs for Ga., Sept. 24, 1735; arriv. in Ga., Feb. 5, 1735/6; chaplain to General Ogelthorpe, Feb. 1735/6-Aug. 1736; at Frederica, St. Simon's Island, Ga., 1736; ret. to England, arriv. there, Dec. 1736; brother of John Wesley; hymn-writer; Ep.-Meth.; d. London, England, Apr. 5, 1788 (bur. Marylebone Par. Chh. yard).

JOHN BENJAMIN WESLEY, A.M., b. Epworth, Lincoln, Eng., June 17, 1703, son of Rev. Samuel and Susannah (Annersley) Wesley; Charterhouse, 1714-1720; matric. Christ Church Coll., Oxford, July 18, 1720, a. 16 yrs.; A.B., 1724, Fellow, Lincoln Coll., Oxford, 1725, A.M., Feb. 6, 1726/7; Ord. 1728; arriv. Ga., Feb. 5, 1735/6; sett. Savannah, Ga., Mar. 14, 1735/6-Dec. 1737; appointed missionary to Ga., Oct. 10, 1735; only Anglican priest in Ga., Sept. 1737-Dec. 1737; embarked for Eng., Dec. 22, 1737 at Charleston, S. C.; preached at King's Chapel, Boston, Mass., 1737; distinguished founder of Methodism; Ep.-Meth.; d. London, England, Mar. 2, 1791.

BARTHOLOMEW ZAUBERBUEHLER, JR., b. St. Gall, Switzerland, Sept. 8, 1719, son of Rev. Bartholomew, Sen. and Elizabeth (Baer) Zauberbuehler; educated at Charleston, S. C., Feb. 19, 1736/7-Nov. 4, 1745; Ord. (Bishop of London), ca. 1745; K.B. Ga. Feb. 4, 1745/6; S.P.G.; sett. Savannah, Ga., 1746-1766; Frederica, Ga., Jan. 22, 1746/7-1766; Londonderry, S. C., 1752-1766; spoke French; Luth.-Germ. Reform.-Ep.; d. Dec. 1766.

JOHN JOACHIM ZUBLY, D.D., b. St. Gall, Switzerland, Aug. 27, 1724, son of David Zubly; stud. at Tuebingen and Halle; A.M., Princeton, 1770, D.D. 1774; Ord. German Reformed Chh., London, England, Aug. 19, 1744; arriv. Ga., 1744; sett. Frederica, St. Simon's Island, Ga., 1744-1747 (E) (and Vernonsburg, 1744-1747); Amelia (Orangeburg) S. C., St. John's Chh., 1747-1749 (GR), Amelia, S. C.,

St. Matthew's Chh., (L) 1747-1749; Purysburg (Jasper) S. C. (GR) 1744-1748; Cainhoy, S. C., (P) 1748-1757; Charleston, S. C., St. John's Chh., (GR) 1749-Jan. 27, 1759; Wappetaw, S. C., Chh. at Wando Neck, (C) 1753-1759; Savannah, Ga., 1760-1778; memb. Provincial Congress, Ga., 1775; delegate, Continental Congress, 1775-1776; banished from Ga., 1777; German-Reformed but also preached in Lutheran, Congregational, Presbyterian and Episcopal churches, as noted above; d. Savannah, Ga., Aug. 26, 1781.

THE COLONIAL CHURCHES OF MARYLAND, 1629-1776

1675 All Faiths' Parish (St. Mary's) (E)
1682 All Hallows' Parish (Anne Arundel) (E)
1692 All Hallows' Parish (Worcester) (E)
1692 All Saints' Parish (Calvert) (E)
1742 All Saints' Parish (Frederick) (E)
1644 Annapolis, Puritan Chh., 1644-1648. X.
1692 Annapolis, St. Anne's Chh. (E)
1745 Antietam (Washington) (Moravian)
1752 Antietam " (Germ. Bapt.)
1754 Antietam " (L)
1756 Antietam " (GR)
Apple's Chh., see Mechanicstown.
1744 Augustine Parish (Cecil) (E)
Baird's Church, see Cavetown.
Baltimore, see Rock Creek.
1692 Baltimore (Baltimore) St. Paul's Chh. (E)
1720 Baltimore " St. Peter's Chh. (RC)
1750 Baltimore " 1st G.R. Chh. (GR)
1757 Baltimore " (L)
1761 Baltimore " (P)
1769 Baltimore " (B)
1770 Baltimore " 2nd G.R. Chh. (GR)
1763 Beaver Creek (Washington) Mt. Zion Chh. (Mennonite)
Berlin, see Buckingham.
Bethany Chh., see Rockville.
1769 Bethel (Harford) Upper Node Forest Chh. (P)
1716 Bethesda (Montgomery) Cabin John Chh. (P)
1719 Bladensburg (Prince George) (P)
Boarman Estate, see Zekiah Swamp Creek.
1704 Bohemia (Cecil) St. Xavier's Chh. (RC)
1684 Bohemia Manor (Cecil) (Labadist)
1723 Bohemia Manor " (P)
1723 Broad Creek. (P)
Broad Creek, see Piscataway Parish.
1743 Buckingham (Worcester) At Berlin, Eastern Shore. (P)
Cambridge, see Great Choptank Parish.
1750 Cardiff (Harford) (P)
1764 Carrollton (Frederick) (RC)
1770 Cavetown (Washington) Baird's Chh. (GR)
1700 Chapel Point (Charles) St. Ignatius' Chh., St. Thomas' Manor (RC)

THE COLONIAL CHURCHES OF MARYLAND 95

1765 Chester Parish (Kent) St. Paul's Chh. (E)
1737 Chestertown (Kent) (P
     Chestnut Hill, see St. Luke's Parish.
1742 Chestnut Ridge (Baltimore) Sater's Baptist Chh., Fall's Road. (B)
     Christ Chh., see King and Queen (St. Mary's).
1629 Christ Church Parish (Queen Annes) (E)
1675 Christ Church Parish (Calvert) At Port Republic. (E)
1768 Church Hill (Frederick) (L)
1738 Churchville (Harford) At Deer Creek. (P)
     Chh. of the Assumption, see St. Inigoes.
1745 Conococheague (Washington) (Moravian)
1747 Conococheague   "   St. Paul's Chh. (GR)
1770 Conococheague   "   St. Paul's Chh. (L)
1770 Conococheague   "   (Germ. Bapt.)
     Copley Parish, see St. John's Parish, Baltimore.
1692 Coventry Parish (Somerset) (E)
1732 Creagerstown (Frederick) (L)
1747 Creagerstown   "   (GR)
1742 Deer Creek (Harford) St. Joseph's Chh. (RC)
     Deer Creek, see Churchville.
     District of Columbia, see Rock Creek Parish.
1697 Doncaster (Talbot) (RC) X.
1692 Dorchester Parish (Dorchester) (E)
1684 Durham Parish (Charles) At Nanjemoy. (E)
1752 East Nottingham (Cecil) (P)
1720 Elk (Cecil) The Rock. (P)
1760 Emmitsburg (Frederick) At Tom's Creek. (P)
1757 Emmitsburg (Frederick) Elias Chh. (L)
     Fair Hill, see Rock.
     Falls Road, see Chestnut Ridge.
1743 Ferry, The (Worcester) (P)
1774 Fishing Creek (Dorchester) (P)
1770 Forest Glen (Montgomery) (RC)
     Franciscan Chapel, see Newport.
1730 Frederick (Frederick) (L)
1747 Frederick   "   (GR)
1770 Frederick County. (Meth.)
1763 Fredericktown (Frederick) St. Stanislaus' Chh. (RC)
1773 Fredericktown   "   (B)
1770 Funkstown (Washington) (GR)
     Garrison Forest, see St. Thomas' Parish.
1756 Glade (Frederick) (GR)
1758 Graceham (Frederick) (Moravian)
1773 Graceham   "   Monocacy Meeting. (Mennonite)
1692 Great Choptank Parish (Dorchester) At Cambridge. (E)
     Guilford, see Queen Caroline Parish.
1770 Hagerstown (Washington) St. John's Chh. (L)
1770 Hagerstown   "   (GR)

96 THE COLONIAL CHURCHES OF MARYLAND

	Hagerstown, see St. John's Parish.
1754	Harford (Harford) (B)
	Herring Creek, see St. James Parish.
	Hickory Mission, see Rock Creek.
1771	Holy Trinity Chh., Eldersburg (Carroll) (E)
	Indian Mission, see Patuxent.
1774	Jerusalem (Harford) (P)
	Jesuit Chapel, see Newport.
1737	Kent (Kent) At Chestertown. (P)
1639	Kent Island (Queen Annes) (RC) X.
1650	King and Queen Parish (St. Mary's) Christ Chh. (E)
	Kittatinny Mt. Chh., see Middletown.
	Kreiger's Chh., see Westminster.
	Leonardstown, see St. Andrew's Parish, and St. Mary's City.
1730	Lower West Nottingham (Cecil) Lower Octoraro Chh. (P)
1760	Manchester (Carroll) Zion Chh. (L)
1760	Manchester (Carroll) (GR)
	Manokin, see Princess Anne.
1765	Mechanicstown (Frederick) Apple's Chh. (L)
1765	Mechanicstown " Apple's Chh. (GR)
1769	Meekin's Neck (Dorchester) (RC)
1755	Middletown (Frederick) (L)
1755	Middletown " Zion or Kittatinny Mt. Chh. (GR)
	Monie, see Somerset Parish.
	Monkton, see St. James's Parish
1738	Monocacy (Frederick) (Germ. Bapt.)
1743	Monocacy " (L)
1745	Monocacy " (Moravian)
1747	Monocacy " (GR)
	Monocacy, see Graceham.
	Mount Calvary Chh., see Sharpsburg.
1714	Mount Paran (Baltimore) (P)
	Mount Zion Chh., see Beaver Creek.
	Nanjemoy, see Durham Parish.
1674	Newport (Charles) Franciscan Chapel. (RC) X.
1697	Newport " Jesuit Chapel. (RC) X.
1661	Newtown (St. Mary's) St. Francis Xavier's Chh. (RC)
1760	New Windsor (Carroll) Sam's Creek Chh. (Meth.)
1766	New Windsor " (L)
1706	North Elk Parish (Cecil) St. Mary Anne's Chh. (E)
1692	North Sassafras Parish (Cecil) St. James's Chh. (E)
1700	Nottingham. (7th Day Bapt.)
	Oakland, see Glade.
1773	Old Seneca (Montgomery) (B)
1716	Oxford (Talbot) (E)
1715	Patapsco (Anne Arundel) (P)
1692	Patapsco Parish (Baltimore) (E)
1647	Patuxent (Prince George) Indian Mission. X. (RC)
	Patuxent, see Upper Marlborough.

THE COLONIAL CHURCHES OF MARYLAND

	Piney Creek, see Taneytown.
1756	Pipe Creek. (GR)
1761	Pipe Creek. (P)
1692	Piscataway Parish (Prince George) St. John's Chh., Broad Creek. (E)
1709	Pitts Creek (Somerset) (P)
	Pocomoke Chh., see Rehoboth.
	Poplar Hill, see St. Mary's City.
	Port Republic, see Christ Chh. Parish.
1641	Port Tobacco (Charles) St. Ignatius' Chh. (RC)
1692	Port Tobacco Parish (Charles) (E)
1726	Prince George Parish (Montgomery) (E)
1685	Princess Anne (Somerset) Manokin Chh. (P)
1736	Princess Anne " New Side Chh. (P)
	Princess Anne, see Somerset Parish.
1774	Queen Anne (Talbot) (P)
1704	Queen Anne's Parish (Prince George) St. Barnabas' Chh. (E)
1728	Queen Caroline Parish (Howard) St. John's Chh. (E)
1758	Queenstown (Queen Annes) St. Mary's Chh. (RC)
1683	Rehoboth (Somerset) Pocomoke Chh. 1st Pres. Chh. in Am. (P)
1741	Rock (Cecil) At Fair Hill. (P)
	Rock, The, see Elk.
1726	Rock Creek Parish. Now Washington, D. C. (E)
1720	Rock Creek (Harford) Hickory Mission. (RC)
1761	Rockville (Montgomery) Bethany Chh. (P)
	Rocky Hill, see Woodsborough.
1744	St. Andrew's Parish (St. Mary's) At Leonardstown. (E)
	St. Anne's Chh., see Annapolis.
1692	St. Ann's Parish (Anne Arundel) (E)
1744	St. Augustine Parish (Cecil) (E)
	St. Barnabas's Chh., see Queen Anne's Parish.
	St. Benjamin's Chh., see Westminster.
	St. Francis Borgia's Chh., see Whitemarsh.
	St. Francis Xavier's Chh., see Newtown.
1671	St. George's Parish (Harford) At Spesutia. (E)
	St. George's Chh., Poplar Hill, see St. Mary's City.
	St. Ignatius' Chh., see Chapel Point.
	St. Ignatius' Chh., see Port Tobacco.
1638	St. Inigoes (St. Mary's) Chh. of the Assumption. (RC)
1692	St. James' Parish (Anne Arundel) At Herring Creek. (E)
1770	St. James' Parish (Baltimore) At Monkton. (E)
1683	St. John's Parish (Baltimore) Copley Parish. (E)
1700	St. John's Parish (Washington) At Hagerstown. (E)
1748	St. John's Parish (Caroline) (E)
	St. John's Chh., see Hagerstown.
	St. John's Chh., see Queen Caroline Parish.
	St. John's Parish (Baltimore) see Piscataway Parish.
1764	St. Joseph's Parish (Talbot) (RC)

98   THE COLONIAL CHURCHES OF MARYLAND

1728 St. Luke's Parish (Queen Annes) At Church Hill. (E)
St. Luke's Chh., see Wye Mills.
1742 St. Mary Anne's Parish (Cecil) (E)
St. Mary's Chh., see Queenstown.
St. Mary Anne's Chh., see North Elk Parish.
1634 St. Mary's City (St. Mary's) (RC) X.
1650 St. Mary's City   "   St. George's Chh., Poplar Hill. (E)
1725 St. Mary's Whitechapel Parish (Caroline) (E)
1672 St. Michael's Parish (Talbot) At St. Michael's. (E)
1692 St. Paul's Parish (Prince George) (E)
1692 St. Paul's Parish (Kent) (E)
1692 St. Paul's Parish (Queen Annes) (E)
St. Paul's Chh., see Baltimore.
St. Paul's Chh., see Chester Parish.
St. Paul's Chh., see Conococheague.
1692 St. Peter's Parish (Talbot) (E)
St. Peter's Chh., see Baltimore.
St. Stanislaus's Chh., see Fredericktown.
St. Stephen's Chh., see North Sassafras Parish.
1692 St. Stephen's Parish, Cecilton (Cecil) (E)
1742 St. Thomas' Parish (Baltimore) At Garrison Forest. (E)
St. Thomas's Manor, see Chapel Point.
St. Xavier's Chh., see Bohemia.
1710 Salisbury (Wicomico) Wicomico Chh. (P)
Sam's Creek Chh., see New Windsor.
Sater's Bapt. Chh., see Chestnut Ridge.
1750 Sharpsburg (Washington) Mt. Calvary Chh. (L)
1750 Sharpsburg   "   (GR)
Sharpsburg, see Antietam.
1692 Shrewsbury Parish (Kent) (E)
1684 Snow Hill (Worcester) (P)
1692 Somerset Parish (Somerset) Princess Anne and Monie. (E)
South Sassafras Parish, see Shrewsbury Parish
Spesutia, see St. George's Parish.
1682 Stepney Parish (Wicomico) (E)
1763 Taneytown (Carroll) Piney Creek Chh. (P)
1766 Taneytown   "   (GR)
1770 Taneytown   "   (L)
Tom's Creek, see Emmitsburg.
1744 Trinity Parish (Charles) (E)
1770 Troxel's Chh. (GR)
1756 Turkey (prob. Cecil) (GR)
1690 Upper Marlborough (Prince George) On Patuxent River. (P)
Upper Node Forest Chh., see Bethel.
1774 Vienna (Dorchester) (P)
Washington, D. C., see Rock Creek Parish, Md.
1763 Westminster (Carroll) St. Benjamin's or Krieger's Chh. (L)

1763	Westminster (Carroll) St. Benjamin's or Krieger's Chh. (GR)
1692	Westminster Parish (Anne Arundel) (E)
1760	Whitemarsh (Baltimore) St. Francis Borgia Chh. (RC)
	Wicomico, see Salisbury.
1692	William and Mary Parish (Charles) (E)
1650	William and Mary Parish (St. Mary's) (E)
1756	Winter Run (Harford) (B)
1768	Woodsborough (Frederick) Rock Hill Chh. (P)
1768	Woodsborough " (GR)
1768	Woodsborough " Rocky Hill Chh. (L)
1744	Worcester Parish (Worcester) (E)
1717	Wye Mills (Talbot) St. Luke's Chh. (E)
1748	Yellow Springs (Frederick) (B)
1697	Zekiah Swamp Creek (Charles) Boarman Estate. (RC) X.
1770	Zion's Chh., Urbanna (Frederick) (E) X.
	Zion Chh., see Manchester.
	Zion Chh., see Middletown.

FRIENDS MEETINGS IN MARYLAND, 1656-1776

(The present writer is deeply indebted to Mr. Delmar L. Thornbury's excellent article on "The Society of Friends in Maryland," in the *Maryland Historical Magazine*, June, 1934, vol. xxix, pp. 101-115, as well as to the late John McHenry, Esq., of Baltimore, for the gift of two maps which have been very helpful in locating these Friends Meeting Houses and to Mrs. Richard James Leupold of Baltimore for many magazines and periodicals relating to old Maryland churches.)

1679	Annemessex (Somerset)
1679	Bay Side, near Bushwood (St. Mary's)
	Betty's Cove, on Miles Creek (Talbot), site of the first m.h. of Tred Avon Meeting. q.v.
1701	Brick Meeting House, Calvert (Cecil)
	Brockatanorton Bay, see Pacaty Norton.
1736	Bush Creek (Frederick)
1682	Cecil, possibly Cecilton (Cecil)
1672	Chester, Kent Island (Queen Annes)
	Choptank, see Little Choptank.
	Cliffs, now Calvert Cliffs, St. Leonard's Creek (Calvert).
1736	Deer Creek (Harford)
1700	East Nottingham (Cecil)
	Easton, see Tred Avon.
1680	Elk Ridge, near Ellicott City (Howard)
	Ralph Fishbourne's, possibly Wye (Talbot).

1760	Havre de Grace (Harford)
1660	Herring Creek, now Herring Bay (Anne Arundel)
1693	Howell Powsley, possibly Howell's Point (Kent)
1662	Gunpowder, on Gunpowder River (Baltimore-Harford)
1660	Indian Spring (Prince George)
	Island, see Chester.
1662	Joppa (Harford)
1679	King's Creek (Somerset)
1660	Leonard's Creek, The Cliffs (Calvert)
1672	Little Choptank (Dorchester)
1738	Little Falls (Harford)
1679	Marshel Creek, possibly Marshyhope Creek (Dorchester-Caroline)
1746	Monocacy (Frederick)
1679	Monuy, evidently Monie (Somerset)
1679	Muddy Creek (location unknown to present writer)
1679	Mulberry (Baltimore?)
1679	Nassawadox (location unknown, perhaps in Somerset or Worcester, evidently formed by Friends expelled from Northampton Co., Va. in 1660)
1679	Pacaty Norton, i.e. Poquede Norton, now Brockatanorton Bay (Worcester)
1752	North West Fork (Caroline) (Nicholite Friends.)
1730	Nottingham (Cecil)
1700	Octoraro (Cecil)
1679	Patapsco, Baltimore City, m.h., 1714, near Jones Falls, first church built within the limits of the present City of Baltimore, now called Baltimore Meeting.
1746	Patapsco Forest (Baltimore)
1677	Patuxent (Anne Arundel)
1735	Pipe Creek (Frederick)
1679	Queen Anne (Talbot)
1750	Sandy Spring (Montgomery)
1679	Sassafras (Kent)
1679	South River (Anne Arundel)
1679	Transquaking (Dorchester)
1668	Tred Avon, near Easton (Talbot) Eastern Shore; first m.h. at Betty's Cove, before 1672; 2nd m.h., 1693, oldest church building in Maryland today.
1677	Tuckahoe (Caroline), probably near Denton.
1750	Washington, D. C.
1710	West Nottingham (Cecil)
1655	West River Meeting (Anne Arundel)
1672	Wye (Talbot)

Many of these meetings had meeting houses in the years given above. In 1656, there were Quaker meetings at Herring Creek, Rhoad River, South River, Severn River, Brand Neck, Seven Mountains and Kent Island.

THE COLONIAL CHURCHES OF DELAWARE, 1638-1775

N. C., New Castle Co.; Kent, Kent Co., Sussex, Sussex Co.; X, Extinct.

1700 Appoquinimink (N. C.), Presbyterian.
1704 " (N. C.), St. Anne's Chh., Episcopal.
1750 " (N. C.), Roman Catholic Mission.
1763 Blackwater (Sussex), Presbyterian.
1682 Brandywine (N. C.), Friends Meeting.
1720 Brandywine (N. C.), Presbyterian.
1728 Broadkill (Sussex), St. John Baptist Chh., Episcopal. X.
1717 Cedar Creek Hundred (Sussex), St. Matthew's Chh., Episcopal.
1708 Center (N. C.), Friends Meeting, near Centerville.
1730 Christiana Bridge (N. C.), Presbyterian.
1750 Cold Springs (Sussex), Friends Meeting.
1734 Cool Spring (Sussex), Presbyterian.
1667 Crane Hook (N. C.), at Tran Hook, Swedish Lutheran. X
1717 Dagsboro (Sussex), Prince George's Chapel, Episcopal.
1704 Dover (Kent), Christ Church, Episcopal.
1727 " (Kent), Presbyterian.
1743 " (Kent), Moravian Mission. X.
1751 " (Kent), Roman Catholic Mission.
1700 Drawyer's Creek (N. C.), near Odessa, Presbyterian.
1705 Duck Creek (Kent), Friends Meeting.
1723 " " (Kent), Presbyterian. X.
1743 " " (Kent), Moravian Mission. X.
1775* " " (Kent), Episcopal.
1720 Elk River (N. C.), Presbyterian.
1707 George's Creek (N. C.), Friends Meeting.
1769 Georgetown (Sussex), Presbyterian.
1708 Head of Christiana (N. C.), Presbyterian.
1738 Hockessin (N. C.), Friends Meeting.
1728 Indian River (Sussex), St. George's Chapel, Episcopal.
1750 " " (Sussex), Presbyterian. X.
1749 Kenton Hundred (Kent), Old Dutch Creek or Bryn Zion Chh., Baptist.
1685 Laurel (Sussex), Christ Church, Episcopal.
1750 Laurel (Sussex), Presbyterian.
1663 Lewes (Sussex), Mennonite. X.
1691 " (Sussex), Presbyterian.

* or earlier.

1721 Lewes (Sussex), St. Peter's Chh., Episcopal.
1743 " (Sussex), Moravian Mission. X.
1750* " (Sussex), Friends Meeting.
1750* Little Creek (Kent), Friends Meeting.
1720 Lower Brandywine (N. C.), Presbyterian.
1750* Marshy Creek (Sussex), Friends Meeting.
1705 Middletown (N. C.), St. Anne's, Episcopal.
1750 " (N. C.), Forest Chh., Presbyterian.
1700 Milford (Kent), Three Runs Chh., Presbyterian. X.
1740 " (Kent), Christ Chh., Episcopal.
1720 Mill Creek (N. C.), St. James's Chh. at Stanton, Episcopal.
1721 " " (N. C.), White Clay Creek Chh., Presbyterian.
1737 " " (N. C.), Friends Meeting
1772 " " (N. C.), St. Mary's Chapel at Coffee Run, Roman Cath. X.
1772 Mill Creek (N. C.), St. John's Chapel at Mt. Cuba, Roman Catholic.
1740 Mispillion (Kent), Christ Chh., Episcopal. X.
1750* " (Sussex), Cedar Creek Meeting, Society of Friends.
1727 Murderkill (Kent), Presbyterian.
1750* " (Kent), Friends Meeting.
1688 Newark (N. C.), Friends Meeting.
1710 " (N. C.), Welsh Tract or Pencader Chh., Presbyterian.
1642 New Castle (N. C.), 1st Chh., Swedish Lutheran, became Dutch Reformed.
1654 New Castle (N. C.), 1st Chh., Dutch Reformed, became Presbyterian.
1700 New Castle (N. C.), 1st Chh., Presbyterian.
1678 " " (N. C.), Immanuel Chh., Episcopal.
1705 " " (N. C.), Friends Meeting.
1758 Pencader (N. C.), Associate Presbyterian.
1703 Pencader Hundred (N. C.), Welsh Tract Church, Baptist.
1710 " " (N. C.), Presbyterian, at Glasgow.
1727 Pigeon Run (N. C.), Presbyterian.
1722 Red Clay Creek (N. C.), Mill Creed Hundred, Presbyterian.
1742 St. George's (N. C.), Presbyterian.
1733 Smyrna (Kent), Presbyterian. X.
1740 " (Kent), St. Peter's Chh., Episcopal.
1750 Taylor's Bridge (N. C.), Forest Chh., Presbyterian.
1775* Thoroughfare Neck (Kent), Presbyterian.
1708 White Clay Creek (N. C.), Presbyterian.
1745 " " " (N. C.), New Side Presbyterian. X.
1772 " " " (N. C.), at Stanton, Friends Meeting.
1638 Wilmington (N. C.), Old Swedes Chh., Swed. Luth., became Episcopal.
1737 Wilmington (N. C.), Presbyterian.

1738 Wilmington (N. C.), Friends Meeting.
1769   "   (N. C.), Asbury Chh., Methodist.
1774   "   (N. C.), 2nd Presbyterian Chh.
1775* Forest Chh., Sussex Co., Episcopal. Possibly listed above.
1775* St. Paul's Chh., Kent Co., Episcopal.   "   "   "

THE COLONIAL CHURCHES OF GEORGIA, 1733-1776

1750 Augusta, St. Paul's Chh. (E)
1751 Bethany. (L)
1767 Briar Creek. (P)
1773 Buckhead (Green). (B)
1773 Buckhead. (P)
1735 Darien (McIntosh). (P)
1734 Ebenezer. (L) (Near Savannah)
1739 Frederica, St. Simon's Island. (E)
1751 Goshen (Lincoln). (L)
1767 Goshen. (B)
1772 Kiokee Creek (Columbia). (B)
1752 Midway (Liberty). (C)
1773 New Savannah. (B) Botsford Chh.
1773 St. George's Parish. (E)
1766 St. John's Parish. (E)
1743 St. Simon's Island. (L)
1733 Savannah. (E) Christ Church.
1736 Savannah. (Moravian)
1756 Savannah. (P)
1759 Savannah. (L)
1767 Sunbury (Liberty). (P)
1759 Tuckaseeking. (7th Day Bapt.)
1771 Tuckaseeking. (B)

SUMMARY OF THE COLONIAL CLERGY AND COLONIAL CHURCHES OF MARYLAND, DELAWARE AND GEORGIA

	Churches				Clergy			
	Md.	Del.	Ga.	Total	Md.	Del.	Ga.	Total
Episcopal	57	18	5	80	175	35	15	225
Presbyterian	34	32	6	72	43	50	5	97
Society of Friends	45	16		61	17	2		19
Roman Catholic	22	4		26	112	1		113
German Reformed	21			21	13		2	15
Lutheran	17		5	22	15		8	23
Baptist	7	2	5	14	4	8	4	16
Moravian	4	3	1	8	15	8	2	25
Swedish Lutheran		3		3		15		15
German Baptist	3			3	5			5
Mennonite	2	1		3	2	1		3
Methodist	2	1		3	13	2	2	17
7th Day Baptist	1		1	2	5		2	7
Dutch Reformed		1		1		5		5
Labadist	1			1	1			1
Congregational	1		1	2	1			1
Total	217	81	24	322	421	127	39	587*

* This number does not count the service in other denominations of the 4 Episcopalians, 6 Presbyterians, 3 Lutherans, 2 Moravians, 3 Methodists, and 1 Congregationalist, a total of 21 clergymen, who served in more than one denomination.